Maureen
Best Wishes
& Thanks

Matt Wrack
April 2019

"When all is said and done, firefighting comes down to this:
that a small number of firefighters will go into a darkened,
smoke-logged building not knowing what they are going to meet,
having faith in each other, in the long run being prepared to
risk their lives to save the lives of other people. No matter what
transformation we effect in the fire service, firefighting in its final
stages remains just that, and we do not forget it."

John Horner, General Secretary, Fire Brigades Union, 1939-1964

Firefighters and their union
The first 100 years
1918 - 2018

Book design: Lisa Irving
Picture editor: Anna Zych

First published in 2018 by the Fire Brigades Union, Bradley House,
68 Coombe Road, Kingston, Surrey KT2 7AE
www.fbu.org.uk

Printed and bound in Great Britain by iPrint

ISBN 978-0-9930244-7-4

Picture credits
Getty: front cover, pp10, 13, 16, 19, 31, 49, 59, inside back cover;
Rep Digital: pp56, 63, 77, 90, 96, 98; Mary Evans Picture Library: inside front
cover, pp4, 20, 22, 24, 26, 27, 28, 29, 64, inside back cover;
PA: pp68, 74, 74, 75, 78, 80, 81, 84, 86, 87, 91, 92, 93, 102;
Mirrorpix: pp30, 33, 36, 39, 45, 50, 51, 52, 54, 66, 70, inside back cover;
Reuters: p81; Andrew Wiard: p82; Tim Smith/Panos: p88;
London News Pictures: p103; Jonathan Buckmaster: p99;
Paul Wood: p101; Brenda Prince Format Archives: p72;
Mark Thomas: inside front cover, p8; Geoff Franklin: inside front cover, p71;
Stefano Cagnoni: inside front cover, p94; Courtesy of Glasgow City Archives:
p58; Courtesy of Northern Ireland Fire Service: inside front cover, p73;
Courtesy of Essex Fire Museum: pp17, 34, 46, 53; Courtesy of London Fire
Brigade: pp14, 69; Courtesy of West Midlands Fire and Rescue Service: p97;
Alamy: p35; Lauren Hurley: p8, 107; Jess Hurd: p106 Courtesy of Dorothy
Macedo: p41; Courtesy of Norfolk Fire Museum: p44; Andy Hall: p76.

Terminology: in this book we use the term firefighter unless specifically
quoting from documentation where the term fireman is used.

FIREFIGHTERS AND THEIR UNION

THE FIRST 100 YEARS | 1918-2018

BY FRANCIS BECKETT

Firefighters putting out fires
at the height of the Blitz,
Eastcheap, London, 1940

CONTENTS

PREFACE

ONE HUNDRED YEARS OF SERVICE, STRUGGLE AND SOLIDARITY

THIS BOOK celebrates one hundred years of the Fire Brigades Union and its members. We are rightly proud that our industry specific union has lasted a century. But our plans and preparations for 2018 were as much about planning for the future as they were about looking to the past. Throughout our centenary year we have sought to set out the ups and downs of our history, our achievements and our setbacks. We have also reminded ourselves and others that over these ten decades, it has been the Fire Brigades Union (FBU) which has consistently put forward a vision for developing and improving our fire and rescue service. We have made much progress. But when we have been ignored in debates on fire policy, it has often been terrible tragedies which have brought home the harsh realities of the warnings we have made.

This is the story of the men and women who have built the Fire Brigades Union and at the same time have shaped the profession and the service they worked in. In preparing for the centenary we found many fascinating, moving and powerful stories. Unfortunately there are so many we can only reflect on some in this book. So the stories set out in the following pages tell the story but they only tell part of it. The names mentioned and the incidents reported are representative of a wider history; of the hundreds of thousands who have served in the fire service and have been part of building the Fire Brigades Union. We owe a huge debt to all those who went before us.

I hope you will find the account set out in the following pages interesting and inspiring. I hope that FBU members reading it will be proud of their union and what it has fought for. I hope that others will find some insight into the heart of the FBU and its members. Our union is very much shaped by the jobs our members do and the service they deliver. The fire and rescue service – and those working in it – have suffered unprecedented attacks in the past decade and a half. But we have not given up and nor shall we. It remains a service to be proud of and to be defended. The FBU remains determined to do so.

Matt Wrack

Matt Wrack, General Secretary, Fire Brigades Union

CHAPTER ONE
PROFESSIONALISING THE FIRE SERVICE

n four days, the 1666 Great Fire of London consumed 13,200 houses, 87 parish churches, St Paul's Cathedral, most civic buildings and the homes of 70,000 of the City's 80,000 inhabitants. London did not see devastation like that again until 1940.

Towards the end of the fire, the militia blew up some taller buildings to create firebreaks. If they had done it earlier, the fire might have been much less devastating, but lord mayor Sir Thomas Bloodworth forbade it.

So, after the fire, a "skilful citizen" was appointed to advise the lord mayor, in the event of fire, which houses should be blown up. This was the first victory in the battle to professionalise the fire service – a battle which, for the last 100 years, has been the business of the Fire Brigades Union.

Insurance companies started employing firefighters, to protect property they insured. Then they began to share their equipment, and in the 1880s this gave London its first fire brigade, the London Fire Engine Establishment (LFEE). It only protected property, so a charity was set up later, maintained by voluntary contributions, to protect people: the Society for the Protection of Life from Fire.

The world's first municipal fire service was established in Edinburgh in 1824 by James Braidwood. It soon proved its worth in Edinburgh's great fire that year, which destroyed much of the old part of the city.

Braidwood believed that a city needed a professional firefighting force, independent of any other agency, such as the police. Birmingham found this out the hard way. A badly bungled operation to extinguish a house fire, in which four people died, caused the city to separate its police and firefighting forces in 1879.

Braidwood also introduced protective uniforms, training for firefighters and a scientific approach to firefighting.

His reputation spread south, and he was asked to head the LFEE. In London he led the assault on a massive warehouse fire in Tooley Street in 1861. The LFEE sent 14 fire engines, but they were hampered by the difficulty of getting a supply of water – the Thames was at low tide.

The fire drew a crowd of more than 30,000 spectators from all over the city. Vendors of ginger beer, fruit and other refreshments recorded a roaring trade, and pubs remained open throughout the night during the two weeks it took to extinguish the fire.

While Braidwood distributed brandy to his firefighters to combat fatigue, the front section of a warehouse collapsed on top of him, killing him instantly. Braidwood's funeral – his belt, axe and helmet on top of the coffin, which was carried by a fire engine – became a model for the funerals of firefighters who have died doing their duty.

The Tooley Street fire concentrated minds, and the next year the insurance companies told the Home Secretary they could no longer be responsible for the fire safety of London. The result was the Metropolitan Fire Brigade Act of 1865. London followed Edinburgh's example and set up the Metropolitan Fire Brigade, funded by ratepayers, the Treasury and insurance companies and headed by Captain Eyre Massey Shaw.

Shaping the service: professionalism to unionism

Shaw was a buccaneering, charismatic figure with his own ideas about how things should be done, and these ideas shaped London's fire brigade and influenced brigades all over the country. Like Braidwood, he thought seamen made the best firefighters, and up to 1899 only seamen were accepted into the London brigade.

These two men, Braidwood and Massey Shaw, more than any other individuals, were responsible for creating a dedicated fire service for Britain's cities, and for shaping the service as it entered the twentieth century. They brought professionalism, but they also brought an autocratic military style. Fire stations at the beginning of the twentieth century were run like ships on dry land, and Britain's firefighters were treated as though they were sailors.

The London firefighter had one day's leave in 15. He was on duty night and day, confined to the station, where he slept in a dormitory, or a flat. He was a prisoner in the fire station, with little or no social life. Courting was done in a corner of the appliance room.

Previous page A firefighter and his bride, after their marriage in Wanstead, then part of Essex, August 1928

Facing page The funeral procession of Captain Eyre Massey Shaw, August 1908, a firefighter who formed the Metropolitan Fire Brigade in 1866 and served as its chief officer

Above Often referred to as the greatest fire since the Great Fire of London, the Tooley Street fire began on 22 June 1861 at Cotton's Wharf, where many warehouses were situated. The London Fire Engine Establishment (LFEE) attended the fire, which spread quickly through the warehouses as the doors which separated storage rooms had been left open. A total of 14 fire engines, including a steam fire engine and a floating engine, were all at the scene of the fire

THE BATTLE FOR RECOGNITION BEGINS

The fire service journal *Fire and Water* was horrified that firefighters wanted a trade union, writing in 1913: "We have been wont to regard our firefighters as something more than daily toilers; their calling as higher and nobler than that of the labourer or mechanic… To learn after all that our idol is of clay; that the firemen whom the County Councillors and the people of London have delighted to honour, are willing, if not anxious, to step down to the level of the everyday worker; to forget the dignity and responsibility of their position; to enlist the aid of paid agitators – all that is indeed humiliating."

When he was not fighting fires, he was being drilled by former naval officers, or cleaning equipment, scrubbing floors and polishing brass. There was strict navy-style discipline, drilling, smart uniforms and brass helmets. If the firefighter argued, he could have his pay docked or his leave cancelled.

As historian Victor Bailey put it, for professional firefighters across the country, "habits of obedience and sentiment were instilled by paramilitary regimes," so it's little wonder that "firemen did not readily think in collective terms."

And yet, early in the new century, they started to think about bettering their conditions by joining a trade union.

The trade union movement they joined was expanding fast, from 750,000 in 1888 to six-and-a-half million by 1918. Edwardian England displayed a stark contrast between great wealth and desperate poverty: filthy, teeming slums rubbed shoulders with ostentatious riches, and those at the bottom of the economic heap were making it clear that this situation would no longer be accepted.

Strikes had brought improvements for dockers and others, and in 1900 trade unions formed the Labour Representation Committee (LRC) – the origin of today's Labour Party – to be their political voice.

The next year the railway trade unions were fined £23,000, a massive sum in those days, as compensation to the employers for calling a strike. The Taff Vale judgement effectively made strikes illegal, since employers could recoup the cost of lost business from the unions.

In 1905 some London firefighters joined a trade union, the Municipal Employees Association (MEA), which soon boasted 500 firefighter members.

The next year, the Conservative government was defeated in the great Liberal landslide that brought to 10 Downing Street Sir Henry Campbell-Bannerman, a prime minister who was sympathetic to trade unions and the workers they represented, and who could see that unions were going to be a power in the land whether the government liked it or not. Also entering Parliament were no fewer than 29 MPs from the LRC, who constituted the first ever Parliamentary Labour Party.

The way seemed clear for unions to take up their members' grievances, and the MEA asked for more rooms for married firefighters. London's chief fire officer thought this request "extremely prejudicial to the discipline of the Brigade".

In Northampton, after their supper beer was withdrawn, firefighters threatened to refuse to go to night fires. A strike over wages won a small improvement in Whaley Bridge, Derbyshire. But in London a firefighter could not take up grievances on behalf of his colleagues – that was considered a breach of discipline.

Compromise and progress: Jim Bradley's vision

Enter the first great figure in fire brigade trade unionism. Jim Bradley was the son of a station officer in London's fire brigade, so he knew the firefighters' work, but he didn't do it himself – he was a London park keeper. He could voice the men's grievances without being accused of a breach of discipline.

He was an activist in the MEA, but left it in 1907 to help launch the National Union of Corporation Workers (NUCW), and the firefighters followed him there. He was a socialist as well as a careful and tactical union negotiator, willing to compromise where necessary.

A fillip to recruitment came in 1911, when the London County Council (LCC) gave council employees one day's rest in seven, but excluded firefighters, offering an argument that has become wearisomely familiar over the years: "Although on duty for long hours, the fireman has a fair amount of leisure and is allowed to smoke and to read while on duty."

By the end of 1913, 1,100 of London's 1,300 firefighters were in the NUCW. But the union was not recognised by the LCC, and firefighters were only allowed to petition humbly for improvements to pay and conditions. So they submitted a petition for one day's leave in eight, instead of the present one day in 15; for an end to the rule that sons must leave the tied family home at 18; and for their union to be recognised. The LCC refused all this, offering to bankroll a staff committee.

In 1914, everything was put on hold for four years by the earthquake we know as the First World War. The war killed 37 million people worldwide, and was immediately followed by the deadliest flu epidemic in modern history, which carried off at least another 20 million.

The old politicians expected those young men who had miraculously survived the killing fields to come back to the huge disparities in income that characterised Edwardian England. David Lloyd George's government was content to see dreadfully wounded ex-servicemen begging in the streets of London.

But the young were angry and unforgiving of the old politics. Rudyard Kipling summed up the mood:

If any question why we died
Tell them, because our fathers lied.

Trade-union membership had gone from 4.1 million in 1914 to 6.5 million. Then, in August 1918, London's police went on strike over pay and union recognition.

The police. In wartime. Less than a year after the Russian Revolution, when British ministers entertained fears of a repeat performance here. This was truly alarming, and the government hastened to agree a generous pay deal with the National Union of Police and Prison Officers and no victimisation, though they said trade-union recognition could not be discussed in wartime.

The capital's firefighters watched and learned. They were heartily sick of petitioning humbly and being ignored. Jim Bradley seized the moment, and a strike ballot over union recognition showed a majority. The LCC repeated its offer of a staff committee, but held out against union recognition.

The government appointed Sir George Askwith from the Ministry of Labour to find a solution. Bradley assured Askwith that the London Fire Brigade branch of the NUCW would not get involved in labour disputes outside the fire service, nor in fire service disputes outside London; nor would it foment strikes.

So Askwith decided that London firefighters below the rank of station officer had the right to belong to a union. But employers would not have to talk directly to the union,

Jim Bradley, the firefighters' union leader, told the NUCW conference in 1912: "This revolt of the workers has driven the capitalist class into such a fit of alarm that they are trying various methods to kill the new born strength of the workers…"

SILVERTOWN 1917

In the TNT blast at Silvertown, east London (right), in 1917, firefighter Frederick Sell and sub-officer Henry Vickers were among the 73 men, women and children killed. The blast wrecked the fire station, brought down many houses and was heard in Sandringham, Norfolk, more than 100 miles away. Fires and explosions at munitions factories were common in the First World War. A Faversham explosion in 1916 killed 106 people. It was heard on the French coast, dinner tables shook in London, and plate-glass windows shattered on the seafronts of Essex. A young firefighter, Steve Epps, recalled: "We'd just got the water on it, and up she went." Blown into a dyke and half-buried under shattered timbers, Epps was the only survivor of his group of seven firefighters.

but rather to a "Representative Body" (RB), which would have a "spokesman" from outside the fire service. The assumption was that Bradley would combine the role of spokesman with being secretary of the union, and the RB would concern itself only with welfare and conditions of service.

It fell short of what the firefighters wanted, but their leaders had done better than the police, who never got their independent union. The police union called another strike in 1919, and the government swiftly abolished the union, banned police from ever going on strike again and foisted the no-strike Police Federation on them.

The Askwith award required firefighters to have their own trade union, rather than be members of a general union. So Jim Bradley talked to a benefit society called The Society of London Firefighters (SLF), whose members were mostly privately employed firefighters.

The SLF agreed to become a trade union called the Firemen's Trade Union (FTU), and the FTU had 1,967 members when it opened for business in October 1918. Bradley became assistant secretary, responsible for all industrial relations matters, and general secretary when the incumbent, George Gamble, retired four years later.

The union swiftly negotiated a small increase in pay, and one day's leave in 10 instead of one in 15. In 1919 they got a weekly rest day, and in 1920 14 days' annual leave. The FTU was proving its value to its members very quickly, and aimed to recruit as many as possible of Britain's 3,400 full-time professional firefighters, 1,300 of them in the London Fire Brigade.

BROTHERS IN ARMS

Almost all TUC-affiliated trade unions were called out in the general strike – but not the firefighters. Prohibited from striking under the Askwith award, they had a special dispensation from the TUC, but their executive urged members to give moral and financial support to the strike. Many firefighters volunteered 5% of their wages for the strike fund.

It was hampered by the naval discipline that still prevailed in fire stations – a third of London's firefighters were former sailors, and there was talk of keeping a "disciplined ship". But the FTU was riding the wave of postwar anger and optimism, when a record 45% of the workforce belonged to a union. That wave was about to recede.

The mines, nationalised during the First World War, were denationalised immediately afterwards, much to the disappointment of the miners, who blamed the mine owners' greed and lack of enterprise for the unnecessary harshness of their lives.

Britain needed coal. Getting it out of the ground was backbreaking and dangerous work, and miners worked long hours for little pay in appallingly dangerous conditions. So renationalisation was top of the list of demands put to the government by the 900,000-strong Miners Federation of Great Britain (MFGB), along with reductions in hours and an increase in pay.

But Lloyd George's Conservative-dominated government was having none of it. The mine owners saw their dividends shrinking and resorted to the simple formula of cutting the miners' wages and increasing their hours. So the miners went on strike, but were defeated and returned to work with pay not just reduced but, in many districts, halved.

The FTU knew whose side it was on. From its meagre funds, it gave the MFGB £150. Meanwhile, in 1920 Manchester took a step backwards by merging its police and firefighting services to save money. It made the fire service less professional and less effective, and it made union organisation harder, because "fire-bobbies" were, like all police, prohibited from joining a union.

But that year also saw the Middlebrook Report, chaired by Sir William Middlebrook, a Yorkshire Liberal MP. Middlebrook heard lengthy evidence from Jim Bradley: "The men are just as isolated as if they were at sea… [They] will tell you themselves they get sick and tired of one another's society… of seeing one another's faces and hearing the same yarn over and over again… If you take a woman into a London fire station it is practically condemning her to penal servitude…"

Above Firefighter Harry Coyston, based at Grays fire station, undergoes a training exercise circa 1914

Middlebrook recommended a standard rate of pay and pensions based on that of the police. He called for full pay for the first three months' sickness, free medical attendance (a significant benefit in those pre-NHS days) and retirement at 55. Local fire brigades did not have to adopt Middlebrook's recommendations, but several did.

But the very next year London firefighters had their wages cut by 2.5% for twelve months as an austerity measure.

The push for parity – and a change of name

The link with police pay was salvaged, but two years later the LCC said it wanted to slash a fifth off firefighters' pay and leave police pay intact. The union took the case to an industrial court and won. The FTU affiliated to the Trades Union Congress in 1923 and the Labour Party in 1926.

Wages, including those of firefighters, were being pushed downwards. The minority Labour government of 1924 fell after less than a year in office, to be replaced by a Conservative government headed by Stanley Baldwin, and the mine owners wanted to reduce miners' pay again. MFGB leader Arthur Cook tramped the country with the slogan: "Not a minute on the day, not a penny off the pay" and the general strike in support of the miners began on 3 May 1926.

It collapsed nine days later amid furious recriminations – the miners felt the rest of the trade unions had betrayed them – and a triumphant Conservative government saw its chance to rein in the unions.

Recruitment was falling as disillusion set in, and FTU finances were shaky. Then in 1929 Jim Bradley died suddenly, aged 61. He was succeeded by his assistant general secretary, Percy Kingdom, a former seaman and retired firefighter who had been with the union from the beginning in the Corporation Workers, and had joined the fire service before the Boer War. He was stubborn, hard-working, determined, dour, gruff-voiced and plain-speaking.

It fell to Kingdom, the following year, to guide the union through its first and only name change. In order to remove any doubt that it did not organise outside the fire brigades, the union became known, and has been known ever since, as the Fire Brigades Union (FBU).

The 1931 financial crisis brought down the Labour government, and Labour leader Ramsay MacDonald joined forces with the Conservatives to head a National Government. They won a landslide election victory, and their first act was to cut the pay of all public employees by 10%.

In 1934, Labour took control of the LCC, and the FBU hoped for a more sympathetic hearing at County Hall. But Kingdom found, as Bradley had before him, that the Labour politician who became LCC leader, Herbert Morrison, was not inclined to do the firefighters any favours.

Kingdom wrote in his 1935 message to members: "In my notes of last year I spoke of the shoals likely to be met in our forward march, and now that we have approached open water we find that our allies of former days are besetting this water with mines to prevent our approach to that which is, in my opinion, a perfectly just and legitimate goal." The goal was for the 72-hour week to be reduced to 48 hours, and the mines were being laid by Morrison.

Kingdom pointed out that the hours undermined pay parity with the police, since police did not work anything like those hours. Morrison trotted out the now familiar argument that for: "a substantial proportion of his time" the firefighter was only "available" for work – not actually working. Himself the son of a London policeman, Morrison wrote sarcastically: "I have yet to learn that a policeman has sleeping trestles provided for him during his tour of duty, or that he can go and play billiards during his day duty."

The dispute grew bitter, and Morrison complained of Kingdom: "pursuing tactics of a hostile character against the Labour Party on the Council". Yet, even as he spoke, the need for a professional, properly resourced fire service was being underlined: Hitler came to power in Germany in 1933, and bombing was clearly going to be a feature of any future war.

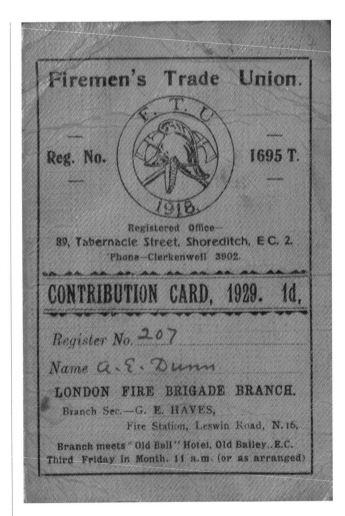

Above A contribution card from 1929, when the union was called the Firemen's Trade Union. The following year the union became known as it is today, the Fire Brigades Union

Opposite A fire crew and tender at London Road fire station, Manchester. The engine was built by John Morris & Sons Ltd, circa 1920

CHAPTER TWO
FROM AUXILIARY FIRE SERVICE TO NATIONAL FIRE SERVICE

n 1937 German bombers supporting Franco in the Spanish Civil War destroyed the town of Guernica and killed 2,000 people. What might such an attack do to London's four million inhabitants, its packed and inflammable warehouses, its maze of narrow streets?

Britain's fire services were not in a fit state to deal with it. The country had about 4,000 full-time firefighters, plus 2,000 policemen engaged on fire duties, in 1,400 independent fire brigades, controlled by local councils. The smallest were controlled by parish councils and consisted of a few part-time firefighters and an ancient pump.

Guernica was a wake-up call. The Home Office told local authorities to draw up air raid precautions and fire protection schemes, and the 1938 Fire Brigades Act made fire protection compulsory for every local authority.

In March 1938, the LCC decided to recruit and train 28,000 wartime auxiliary firefighters for the London Fire Brigade, and set up 360 additional fire stations. Thus was born the Auxiliary Fire Service (AFS).

There were to be two types of auxiliary: part-timers, who did their normal jobs and worked as firefighters when needed; and those who, in the event of war, would give up their jobs and become full-time, paid firefighters.

Eventually there was an AFS in every county and town. Recruiting became quicker after Prime Minister Neville Chamberlain's pact with Hitler at Munich. Chamberlain thought it meant "peace in our time," but many people thought the opposite.

Auxiliary firefighters came from every trade and profession: sailors and solicitors, bricklayers and

fishmongers, milkmen and mechanics, hairdressers and car salesmen.

And some of the recruits were women. Women had not worked in public fire brigades before, though they had been employed by private brigades, and Girton College in Cambridge had an all-women brigade. The women were not originally expected to extinguish fires but to work in control and as drivers and despatch riders. They did, as we now know, so much more.

Many regular firefighters were suspicious of the AFS. AFS people did not have the training and experience of regular firefighters – most of them had just 60 hours' training. Their commanders were not firefighters, but people with what was called a suitable background, which meant the professional classes. They were bound to clash with members of the regular fire service, who knew a great deal more about firefighting and inevitably saw the new influx as a threat to their own professionalism, status, pay and conditions.

AFS people were to be paid £3 a week for men, £2 for women. Most regular firefighters earned more, and naturally feared a levelling downwards.

So many FBU members wanted to keep the AFS out of the union. But a young London firefighter, a member of the union's executive called John Horner, led a faction demanding a very different strategy.

The union, he pointed out, had 3,150 members – but there were to be thousands of AFS firefighters in London alone. "If the AFS was mobilised before the FBU had found a constructive relationship with it, the union would be swamped out of existence," he wrote later.

Horner was just 27, a young idealist in a hurry. The previous year, 1937, he had clashed with Percy Kingdom at the union's annual conference, arguing for trade union education because: "it has been my very bitter experience to listen to my brother trade unionists decrying the efforts and demands put forward by the London busmen in an attempt to reduce their working week."

As the AFS debate was raging, the LCC finally came up with an offer on hours: a 60-hour week. It was not the 48 hours the union wanted, but it was a considerable

4,800 WOMEN

By 1943 there were 4,800 women in the fire service. The FBU had women organisers and was demanding the same conditions for them as for men. An all-female fire station was established in Northumberland because there were no men to do the work.

Above John Horner at first hated the fire service's military-style uniforms and drilling, but: "I came to realise that the strong bond of mutual reliance which characterised the job could be a powerful element in forging a special kind of trade union for a special kind of service"

Facing page Firefighters of the NFS (London Region) at the telephone switchboard of the control room at Lambeth HQ during the Second World War, late 1941

Previous page NFS women undergoing dispatch rider training, 1942. They were widely used to supplement the lines of communication between various headquarters and the incident ground, where telephone lines were unavailable or non-existent

Overleaf Fighting fires at Thames Haven oil tanks during the Second World War, 1940

improvement on the 72 hours firefighters worked at the time, and Percy Kingdom was inclined to accept it. But the LCC hedged the offer around with conditions, chiefly petty disciplinary measures of the sort approved by the LFB chief, a crusty former naval commander, Sir Aylmer Firebrace. So the men followed Horner's lead and rejected it.

Kingdom was due to stand for re-election. Horner said he would stand against him, whereupon Kingdom announced his retirement, nominated as his successor his assistant secretary, Harold Gibbs, an administrator who had never been a firefighter, and persuaded the executive to rule Horner's nomination invalid.

All change: John Horner, union reformer

Horner went on the campaign trail, and the storm he whipped up convinced Kingdom to accept his nomination. Horner won. Kingdom, Gibbs and the only other full-time official resigned.

So Horner started the job with an office, a filing cabinet, a typewriter that he had never learned to use, and not a single member of staff. The executive agreed that he might appoint a typist, with the proviso that no woman should be employed.

John Horner knew what poverty did to people. His father had arrived in London, a 13-year-old orphan, looking for work: "He was to remain an illiterate navvy until, his strength failing, he simply died."

A scholarship to a grammar school led to him becoming a trainee buyer for Harrods. It could have heralded a comfortable life far removed from the privations of his parents, but after a year he left, travelled the world with the Merchant Navy and became a qualified second officer. Failing to find a ship because of the economic crisis of the 1930s, he joined the fire service.

As a seaman, he wrote: "I had seen the unwanted wheat of the prairies of America mixed with tar to fuel dockside locomotives, while starving jobless immigrants wandered the quays and begged for scraps from the hogswill in our galley's shit-bucket." Now he was seeing the dreadful poverty of thirties Britain.

Horner set about recruiting the AFS. It was a highly controversial move. Torn-up membership cards with "traitor" and "sell-out" written on them began arriving at the union's office, and TUC general secretary Walter Citrine told him: "You are attempting the impossible." But FBU membership surged from 3,500 in 1939 to 66,500 in 1940. Horner told the 1940 conference: "Whatever may be the results of this war, the fire service as we knew it in prewar days has gone for good."

Hitler invaded Poland on 1 September 1939. Two days later, Neville Chamberlain declared war. Home Secretary Sir John Anderson made Sir Aylmer Firebrace the new London Regional Fire Officer, and gave his job at the LFB to his deputy, Major Frank Jackson. Firebrace was furious, but it was one of the best decisions Anderson ever made. Jackson quickly formed a working relationship with Horner that shaped the defence of the home front.

For more than a year after the declaration of war, the men and women of the AFS had little to do. Their bosses tried to fill their time, but duties like scrubbing brass seemed a pointless way to spend one's days.

But on 24 August 1940, air attacks on airfields, ports and aircraft factories began. On 5 September the Luftwaffe scored a direct hit at Thameshaven, setting five 2,000-ton oil tanks ablaze.

The fire was far too big for the local brigade to handle alone, and Commander John Fordham came in from the LFB and at once demanded 40 pumps and three fireboats to be sent from London. He was told that local authorisation for the request was required.

Fordham was furious. Firefighters were inches from a dreadful death. If some of the burning oil fell into the pit in which they were working, they would all be fried, and every moment's delay prolonged the danger unnecessarily.

For some arcane reason, the request had to go to the regional commissioner for Essex and East Anglia, who turned out to be the Master of Corpus Christi College, Cambridge. Fordham was told that the Master had retired for the night, and his staff were reluctant to wake him.

Eventually the Master's emissary, a young man in a sports jacket, arrived driving a sports car and stared, horrified, at the blaze. He said he knew next to nothing

GEORGE ARTHUR ROBERTS

Originally from Trinidad, George Arthur Roberts is thought to be Britain's first black firefighter. He fought for Britain in the First World War and saw action in France. After the war, he settled in England and signed up to the NFS, where he was posted at New Cross fire station and later promoted to section leader. In 1944 he was awarded the British Empire medal.

about firefighting, and, as the representative of the sleeping Master, he authorised Fordham to take what action he considered necessary. Fordham ordered the pumps and fireboats.

"I believe that the idea of a national fire service was born in Fordham's mind that night at Thameshaven," wrote Horner. "He became a propagandist for reform and between us we maintained an uneasy contingent alliance for years."

The price of freedom: life during wartime

On 7 September 1940, 364 German bombers, escorted by 515 fighters, followed the Thames Estuary to London. It was the first day of the Blitz.

John Horner stood at the top of Chingford Mount and saw London below, "dark now with the searchlights dimmed as the bombers flew homeward. A few miles to the east of us the very firmament was alive with flame and smoke. The loom of the fires in the docks was seen at Bedford and beyond."

On that first night, 448 people were killed. The bombers came back the next night, and the next. Firefighters became, in Winston Churchill's words, "heroes with grimy faces".

They hardly felt treated like heroes, though. "The complete lack of care for the auxiliaries in many brigades was nothing short of criminal," wrote the FBU's AFS national officer Peter Pain. "In the vast majority of cases, stations had atrociously bad living conditions." Many had no cooking or heating facilities, and others had no beds – men slept on bare boards – and primitive toilet arrangements. "Mac" Young in Paddington found that his sub-station, a Great Western Railway recreation hall, wasn't ready, and he and his 24 AFS colleagues bedded down amid the straw with 200 restless GWR horses.

Major Jackson arranged an informal meeting between Horner and Sir Arthur Dixon, head of fire services at the Home Office. As Horner wrote later: "I said that we had four mobile fire service canteens for the whole of London. Men cut off from help had been known to drink water from the Thames… Men came back to their makeshift depots,

Above The Blitz in London, 1940. Firefighters clearing debris at what was their sub-fire station in Hugh Myddleton Primary School, Finsbury, EC1. The building took a direct hit from a high explosive bomb

Facing page Getting what sleep was possible during the hectic days and nights of enemy bombing during the Blitz: firefighters with bunk beds put up in the basement from salvaged materials, at New Cross sub-station, Monson Road, south-east London, circa 1940

sodden, tired out and filthy, with no means of drying their only uniform and liable to be called out again…

"True, a week or two earlier the government had relieved injured men in hospital of their liability to contribute towards the cost of their medical treatment, but I told him that discharging injured men from the service after three weeks, and sending them to seek help from the assistance board, was doing more to destroy the morale of the AFS than any bombing."

Jackson later said that the fire service could not have got through the war without the union's help and co-operation, while Horner wrote of Jackson: "He received no honours, no knighthood, but 'Gentleman Jackson' deserves honourable mention."

On 16 September Jackson reported that the fire service had already lost two officers, 19 firefighters and one firewoman. Another 11 were missing, presumed dead; 151 men, three women and one youth were seriously injured. Firefighting had become one of the most high-risk of all wartime occupations.

AFS man Harry Errington was in a Soho basement that firefighters used as an air raid shelter and rest area when a bomb struck and all three floors collapsed, killing 20 people, including six firefighters who had been trying to sleep on the hard concrete floor, their uniforms serving as

HONOURING THE HEROES

One of the first firefighters to die in the Blitz was 44-year-old station officer Gerry Knight. His thigh-length boots served to identify his few remains. AFS messenger Betty Barrett told writer Cyril Demarne: "He was a lovely man, so kind to us girls. I broke my heart over the news and cried for days. He used to smoke Gold Flake and always gave us a cigarette. He knew we only earned £2 a week and I kept remembering those little kindnesses."

Eleven years later, in 1953, FBU national official Mark Bass found Gerry Knight's widow living in "intolerable conditions". He badgered the LCC Housing Committee until she was given a flat at Tooley Street Old Fire Station. "The FBU never forgets a comrade," reported *Firefighter*.

pillows. As Harry dashed for the emergency exit, fierce fires all round him, he heard the cries of a comrade whose legs were trapped by heavy masonry.

Wrapping a blanket around his head and shoulders, Harry dug the injured man out with his bare hands and dragged him up the narrow staircase and out to the street. Despite severe burns to his hands and the danger of the basement collapsing, he went back to rescue a second man pinned against a wall by a heavy radiator, and carried him to safety.

Digging deep: battling the Blitz

Harry's burns failed to heal in the prescribed 13 weeks, so he was discharged from the AFS. "He was sacked on the same day that he received his citation from Buckingham Palace [for the George Cross] and a letter from the King," wrote John Horner in disgust. It had taken a strident campaign, orchestrated by Horner, even to get Errington paid for those 13 weeks.

Born in 1910 to Polish immigrants Solomon and Bella Ehrengott, Harry Errington had joined the AFS three weeks before war broke out, thinking of his 20 Jewish relatives in Poland. He later learned that they were all murdered in the Holocaust. After the war, Harry went back to his trade as a tailor. In 2000, on his 90th birthday, Soho fire station gave a party for him.

Soho fire station was itself bombed. John Horner, who happened to be passing, walked through a huge cloud of smoke and dust to find that a bomb had sliced off the top floor, and the ceiling of the appliance room had collapsed.

"Already the men who had survived were digging into heaped debris. . . . Girls in the control room were badly injured and three LFB men who had been in the mess were dead." He helped his members to search for their colleagues.

After 57 nights of continuous action on London, on 3 November the Germans turned their fire on provincial cities. Birmingham and Bristol had been attacked on 15 October. Now Belfast, Cardiff, Clydebank, Coventry, Exeter, Greenock, Sheffield, Swansea, Liverpool, Hull, Manchester, Portsmouth, Plymouth,

Above Piles of debris outside Soho fire station following an air raid, 7 October 1940

Facing page A field kitchen is set up to feed the London regular and AFS firefighters whose sub-station in Woolwich, south-east London, was seriously damaged during an air raid, 1941

Nottingham, Brighton, Eastbourne, Sunderland and Southampton were to experience heavy air raids and many casualties.

Coventry suffered a devastating attack on the night of 14-15 November, 1940, which destroyed the centre of the city. By 8pm – less than an hour after the first bombs fell – the central fire station had recorded 240 fires. Then the station itself was hit, and accurate recordkeeping became impossible.

The city's own fire service fought the blaze for four hours before reinforcements were sent for. John Horner went with Coventry FBU branch secretary George Dipper to a service for the city's dead in the ruined cathedral, and he retained all his life a clear memory of George Dipper, in his filthy uniform, walking towards the ruin. They both knew that reinforcements had been sent for far too late. Lessons had to be learned.

On the night of Sunday, 29 December, 1940, German aircraft flung down incendiary and high-explosive bombs on the City of London, near St Paul's Cathedral, where buildings were crammed together: offices, churches and warehouses, separated by narrow passages and alleyways.

Firefighters laid a hose from the river to pump in water, but the hose was destroyed by bombs within half an hour. They laid more hose, but the Thames was at a low ebb, and they had to manoeuvre their pumps down stone steps into the soft mud and walk through it, waist deep, to connect hoses to the fireboats. Some pumps became bogged down in the thick mud and had to be abandoned when the tide came in.

While the men manned the pumps, women were driving petrol carriers, canteen vans and staff cars into the thickest parts of the blaze, ensuring that the pumps had petrol to keep going. Driving vans laden with cans of petrol through a hail of bombs and a wall of fire was about as dangerous a job as you could do.

And, when necessary, the women would step out of role to help control the huge, bucking hoses. "With that pressure, there was two feet of metal on the end that would take your head off," recalled firewoman Gladys Gunner. St Paul's was saved, but most of Wren's other churches

Above Bristol, 24 November 1940. Cliff Latchem, an AFS pump driver, recalled the bombing of Bristol: "There was no water in the hydrants as most of the mains supply had been fractured by the bombing so we used the water in the tanks and had pumped them dry by about 11pm… That night, there were 200 people killed and 639 injured. This raid found a lot of faults in the organisation and one of the worst was having to go into the centre of Bristol to report; by the time of the next raid, this had been altered."

Facing page St Paul's Cathedral, illuminated by fires and surrounded by the smoke of burning buildings, 30 December 1940. It became a symbol of British resilience and courage. This is considered one of the most iconic images of the Blitz

were destroyed. Seventeen awards were made for bravery, including four to women who had driven essential vehicles. Fourteen firefighters died.

The last major air raid on London – and the most destructive – was on 10 May 1941. A full moon allowed German bombers to follow the Thames and spot their targets; the low tide meant a desperate shortage of water. Some of London's most important buildings were damaged, including the Houses of Parliament and the British Museum.

Water directed from fireboats rapidly dwindled into thin streams, and fire crews went to public swimming pools, canals, ponds, flooded bomb craters and sewers. Some of the bombs were aimed at firefighters: delayed-action parachute mines fell on the men as they rushed to deal with the fires.

The FBU's new offices in Chancery Lane were destroyed, and for the rest of the war the bombs seemed to follow the FBU around – it was bombed out of offices in Hampstead, then Holborn; and a bomb damaged, but failed to destroy, the union's final wartime home in Bedford Row.

That May night brought into sharp focus the old problem identified by Commander Fordham: how to concentrate firefighting forces quickly where they were needed. The RAF monitoring unit warned Major Jackson in the afternoon that the radio beams used by Luftwaffe bombers to guide them towards their targets

HEROES, WITH NO HEROES' BURIAL

At first, bereaved families of AFS firefighters got nothing, and the fire station had to have a whip-round so that the men were not buried in paupers' graves. The 14 firefighters killed saving St Paul's on 29 December 1940 included AFS men Benjamin Chinnery and Herbert Blundell. Blundell's widow could not afford to bury him, so Chinnery's widow agreed to them being buried together. Since Chinnery did not complete a full week's work, his widow did not receive a full week's pay.

MINUTES OF A MEETING OF THE JOINT EXECUTIVE COUNCIL
of the Professional and A.F.S. Sections of the
FIRE BRIGADES UNION,
held at the offices of the London Trades Council, 24 Thavies Inn London, W.C.1. on WEDNESDAY, 9TH OCTOBER, 1940, at 10.30 a.m.

Present: A.F. ODLIN (President): A. J. CURTIS (Vice--President); L. BOULTON, J. C. BRADLEY, J. BURNS, W. J. JENKINS, S. W. RANDALL, H. S. RICHARDSON, T. W. THOMAS and R. WILLIS.
A.F.S. DELEGATES: K. BAKER, Jenner, L. ROUSE JONES AND M. WASSEY.

The GENERAL SECRETARY (F.J. HORNER) and S. J. MERRELLS (Organising Secretary) were in attendance.

REPORT OF GENERAL SECRETARY. The General Secretary reported the destruction of the Head Office of the Union in Chancery Lane, by enemy action, on the night of the 24th September, 1940. None of the staff had been present at the time, but valuable office records and equipment were lost. An estimate of the property lost - £395. 10. 0. - had been submitted to the appropriate Government department dealing with claims for damage to property in war time.

The General Secretary reported that the outlook was not too gloomy. Financially, the Union was in a very sound position and the past month had shown very good returns from all the branches - professional and A.F.S. Over £540 had been received in contributions in that period.

The Organisation possessed assets totalling £4,349. 6.11

The General Secretary stated that the staff of the Union had reacted in a wonderful fashion to the bombing attacks and the destruction of Head Office. Even in the present difficult circumstances they had laid the foundations of a new system of organisation. In the future all accounts were to be kept in triplicate.

The General Secretary reported the opening of three temporary area offices of the Union in the Metropolitan area, namely, at 13 Park Avenue, Barking, at 101 Broadhurst Gardens, Hampstead and at 50 Epping Way, Chingford. The first two branch offices had actually been opened before the destruction of Head Office and the routine of the Organisation was being carried out daily at those addresses and also at Chingford.

The General Secretary stated that a central registered office in London would be necessary, but, having learned from experience, it was not the intention of the Organisation to "keep all its eggs in one basket". The three temporary area

Left Minutes from an FBU executive meeting dated 9 October 1940, detailing the bombing of the FBU HQ in London

Facing page Bombing of Liverpool during the Blitz, 1941

were set to intersect at West Ham. Making best use of that information was another matter.

The Cabinet realised it had to do what Horner and Fordham had been advocating, and nationalise the fire service. Sir Arthur Dixon at the Home Office had said: "Nationalisation is impossible. The whole of history is against it." But without nationalisation it was impossible to send fire appliances where they were needed on a large scale at great speed.

"If heroism and devotion to duty and self-sacrifice in themselves could constitute an efficient fire service, there would be no need of any reorganisation," Horner told the 1941 FBU conference. "But we know the mistakes that have been made, and we know how we, as firemen, have had to suffer under the inefficiency, the maladministration and the blunders which have been made by local authorities."

Nationalisation: the union finds its voice

The National Fire Service (NFS) was officially created on 18 August 1941, and the benefits were felt at once. The most amateurish of the officers – those who were in charge because of their status in the community – were replaced. No longer might the chain of command involve the town clerk, the chairman of the main drainage committee, or the Master of Corpus Christi College, asleep or awake. A lot of the spit and polish was abolished.

The next month, the union launched the Firemen's Charter, proposing an end to such disciplinary measures as stoppages from pay. It called for full pay while an auxiliary firefighter was sick or injured (which he would get if he was a regular) and a maximum working week of 72 hours (the wartime level was 112 hours). There should be promotion on merit and a national minimum wage. In December the union secured up to 26 weeks' injury pay, and higher wages.

Herbert Morrison, now Home Secretary, talked of using nationalisation as a pretext for outlawing the independent fire service trade union, saying that firefighters would now be Crown servants. But he was persuaded that it was not a good time to get into a fight with the FBU.

The man who persuaded him was probably the Minister of Labour, Ernest Bevin, who shared Horner's low opinion of the Home Secretary. Someone once said to Bevin: "Herbert Morrison's his own worst enemy." "Not while I'm alive 'e ain't," growled Bevin.

Bevin had been Britain's most powerful trade unionist, heading the Transport and General Workers Union. Now Winston Churchill had given him an extraordinary level of central control over the allocation of Britain's manpower. He saw the chance to use this power, not just to help win the war, but to create a new relationship between employer and worker afterwards.

During the war, Bevin's unspoken deal with union leaders was that he would use his position to secure significant improvements in wages and working conditions, while they would try to stave off industrial action that might affect the war effort.

So, in 1942 the government recognised the FBU as the negotiator for firefighters, putting an end to the charade that the Home Office only talked to the 'Representative Body' – though Morrison did manage to set up the National Association of Fire Officers, with Firebrace as its president, to siphon senior men away from the FBU.

The FBU negotiated another pay rise, established its right to speak on the great issues confronting the country and on how the fire service was run, obtained the right to hold union meetings in fire stations and was a key part of the campaign for a second front in the east. It reached an all-time high of 75,000 members.

Altogether, 1942 was quite a year. Jim Bradley could never have dreamed that his union would become such a power in the land.

Above 21-year-old AFS firefighter Gillian Tanner was awarded the George Medal for bravery when she delivered petrol to fire pumps around Bermondsey while the docks were being bombed in 1940

Facing page A Bentley commandeered by the NFS during the Second World War for use as a fire vehicle

CHAPTER THREE
FROM HEROES TO SPIT-AND-POLISH STRIKERS

By 1943, with 32,200 full-time women firefighters and 48,000 part-timers, women made up one in three of the full-time and almost half of the part-time fire service.

A 1941 Home Office memo said that women's duties were telephone and watchroom work, although: "it is not inconceivable that ultimately women may be accepted for observation duties and even as pump operators." The reality was that they were in the thick of the action, doing whatever needed to be done.

In March 1943 the FBU matched its Firemen's Charter with a Firewomen's Charter calling for equal pay. This was rejected by the Home Office, but, after pressure by women MPs, women did get equal compensation if injured by enemy action.

A crisis for the union came with a new rota system, designed to ensure that two thirds of firefighters were always at stations in readiness, and requiring that they worked very long, anti-social hours. Persuasion failed, and Horner told the 1943 FBU conference that wartime industrial action would: "bring into question the operation of trade unionism within a disciplined Service." More than 7,000 firefighters left the union in disgust.

At that conference, to celebrate the union's 25th anniversary, Morrison, Firebrace and Dixon all turned up for the FBU Jubilee Dinner – sausage tart and two veg and treacle pudding – and nailed smiles to their faces.

"Dixon surprised us all with his charm, and Commander Firebrace genuinely tried to unbend before a couple of hundred of his rank and file," reported Horner.

In the summer of 1944 came the doodlebugs. These were pilotless flying bombs launched at London and south-east England, each carrying 150kg of high explosive at 350mph. Some of them caused huge fires. One fell on a Thameside candle works full of paraffin wax, fuel oil and turpentine. Firefighters worked knee-deep in oil and molten wax, and it was a miracle that none of them was killed.

But the flying bombs were Hitler's last throw. During the war 793 firefighters lost their lives on duty, 25 of them women, but the end was in sight. There was a stand-down

parade for AFS people on 18 March 1945, and that evening they were invited to a Cavalcade of Stars at the Albert Hall to hear Vera Lynn, comedian George Robey and others.

One very quick outcome of the end of the war was a sharp decline in the numbers of women employed in the fire service. A Ministry of Labour booklet on fire service employment in 1945 was called *A Man's Job* and by 1948 the number of women was down to 500. In 1949, there was just one woman delegate at the FBU conference, held in July in Whitley Bay. Eve Morrow from Stockport told the conference: "I am aware that it is the policy of the union to support the employment of women in the Fire Brigade, and that it is also the union's policy to go out for equal pay for equal work . . . Firewomen today, rightly or wrongly, feel that the FBU has tended to lose sight of some of the problems that are facing [women] today, but, remembering the good work the union did for us in 1946, when [women] got our last rise in pay – we have not had an increase since – I feel confident they will do the same again."

In December Eve wrote in the FBU magazine *Firefighter*: "Within the union itself I feel that firewomen have insufficient representation, and when conditions of service of firemen are discussed at a higher level, the firewomen's point of view is apt to be bypassed. I feel also that if firewomen could have a representative at all levels in the union and were welcomed to serve at all levels by branch, area and district officials, this bypassing would be avoided."

Women returned to the control rooms and stayed there, mostly, until the pioneering work of the Greater London Council in the early 1980s. By that time, many people had forgotten the huge contribution made by women to the fire service during the Second World War.

A modern fire service: the postwar shake-up

On 5 July 1945, Clement Attlee became Prime Minister at the head of the nation's first Labour government with an overall majority. Labour had 393 seats, the Conservatives 213 and the Liberals 12. With two Communists, one Commonwealth Party and 19 others, Labour had an overall majority of 146.

Above The women delegates at the Fire Brigades Union conference where the union agreed to charter for a campaign for equal pay, 1943

Previous page Camberwell, December 1940. A local resident does her bit during the first attempt to 'burn down' London with high explosives. There were 1,700 fires reported across the capital

Facing page Houses demolished by a flying bomb, southern England, August 1944. Rescue efforts by NFS firefighters and Civil Defence workers to free casualties trapped at the scene soon after the incident

REMEMBERING OUR FALLEN SISTERS

In East London, two young women, friends who had signed up for the AFS together, died in the Blitz within months of each other.

Joan Ridd, 20, was killed when Ricardo Street School took a direct hit. Her friend Hilda Dupree, also 20, was one of 34 to die when a landmine crashed through the school roof at Old Palace School, Bromley-by-Bow, a few months later. Hilda was found clutching "a baby's vest in blue". She'd been knitting while on duty.

Despite rationing and Britain's wrecked economy, it was a moment of wild optimism. There had been such moments before, and disappointment had been swift and bitter. But 1945 was different. Attlee and his ministers set themselves the task of creating a welfare state to a deadline of 5 July 1948, and they achieved it. It was a revolution in the way we lived.

Attlee's government also undertook a huge programme of nationalisation, masterminded by Herbert Morrison. Replacing Morrison as Home Secretary was Chuter Ede, a former teacher who had been a key figure in the passage of the 1944 Education Act. Horner complained to Ede that some AFS men who wanted to stay in the fire service were being turned down, for apparently trivial reasons. Some, for example, did not quite meet the height requirements, which had been relaxed in wartime. But they had been doing the job, under the harshest of circumstances, and Horner told Ede that they should not be thrown out now if they wanted to stay. Ede agreed, and changed the system.

The big question to be settled was the future shape of the fire service. Should it continue as a nationalised service? The FBU thought not. But neither did the union want a return to the prewar system where every local authority had its own fire brigade. It wanted bigger and more efficient units.

Again, the Home Secretary agreed, and the 1947 Fire Service Act returned fire brigades to local authority control. Under this landmark Act, which created the modern fire service, police fire brigades were scrapped, and parish councils were no longer expected to provide fire cover. The number of brigades was drastically reduced, from 1,400 prewar to 135.

A Central Fire Brigades Advisory Council, consisting of government representatives and firefighting organisations, and including seven FBU representatives, was set up to advise the Home Secretary on national policy.

A new national disciplinary procedure would give all those disciplined the right of appeal. Also there was to be a national pension scheme.

A new National Joint Council would deal with wages and conditions, and of the 27 seats on the workers' side, the FBU had 18. One of the council's first decisions was that firefighters should work a 60-hour week – an improvement, but not the 48-hour week that the FBU had wanted since before the war, and not binding on local brigades.

Industrial action and a changing landscape

The war, and the wartime leadership of John Horner, had turned the FBU into a power in the land. The voice of the men and women who fought fires was no longer to be ignored.

For Horner himself, a Labour seat in Parliament in the 1945 landslide followed by a place in the government would probably have been his for the asking, and Herbert Morrison encouraged him to stand for Parliament. Instead he joined the Communist Party.

As a young firefighter in the 1930s, outraged by poverty amidst conspicuous wealth, Horner and many of his generation had been as disappointed with the first Labour Prime Minister, Ramsay MacDonald, as young people of a more recent time became with Tony Blair.

In 1945, Horner said: "I knew that Labour would win the election and I was convinced that in power, it must be reinforced by a strong militant trade union movement and buttressed outside of Parliament by a left-wing socialist party that would join in the building of the new Britain. So I threw in my lot with the Communist Party."

Even with Attlee's Labour Party in power, even with the sympathetic Ede at the Home Office, there was bound to be a falling out sometime. It came when Ede responded to a crime wave by raising police pay, but refused to do the same for firefighters, whose pay was linked with the police. There was, he pointed out, a pay freeze.

The *Firefighter* editorial in October 1951 complained: "The police have had another increase in pay. A big increase… How comes it that the police are singled out for special dispensation, when every other worker is being called upon to exercise restraint…"

Firefighters know, better than anyone, how vital they are in keeping everyone else safe. In 1951 their union had got through its first 33 years without any national industrial action. Even now, when their traditional pay safeguard had

The E.C. Delegation that met Sir Arthur Dixon with regard to the Overseas contingent: Bros. Baker, Dutton, Richardson, Fewkes, Horner, Merrells, Grahl, Murray and Bagley.

Above *Firefighter*, September 1944. Members of the overseas contingent were 'straining at the leash' to go and help the military deal with fires. Representations made by the FBU to the Home Office produced positive results

Facing page Spit-and-polish strike, 1951. Police received an increase in pay but not so firefighters

'CRIME' AND PUNISHMENT

In Manchester during the spit-and-polish strikes, firefighters who had been suspended for refusing to clean floors nonetheless turned out to fight a fire in a rag waste mill. The chief officer retaliated by compelling them to walk back to their stations in full firefighting gear.

been taken away from them, they were not going to walk out of their fire stations.

Their compromise was the so-called spit-and-polish strike – a very limited sort of action, carefully calibrated not to put anyone in danger.

In the second half of 1951 they ran two 48-hour boycotts of routine station duties. Firefighters reported for duty as usual. All fire calls and all other calls for assistance were answered, but training, domestic chores and brass polishing were banned.

So it hit only inessential duties – duties that, as historian David Englander put it: "offended the fireman's image of himself as a skilled worker performing a public service and made him feel undervalued."

It started in London, but within days it included 70% of the service. For the first time in 79 years, Clerkenwell's bell went unpolished.

But while this was going on, the Labour government fell and the Conservatives under Winston Churchill obtained a small but workable parliamentary majority. That seemed to some Conservative-run local authorities a signal that they should put the firefighters' union back in its box. So three Southend firefighters were suspended for refusing to obey orders. A local union official pointed out that the Southend employers were taking the step the firefighters themselves had not taken – removing fire cover – and the three were reinstated the next day.

The spirit of Southend spread. "Men are being broken in rank and others heavily fined. This victimisation is intended to destroy the fighting ability of the union in defence of its members' living standards," said a head-office circular to members.

The *New Statesman* magazine wrote: "This demonstration, which took the form merely of a collective refusal to perform duties unconnected with firefighting, was in fact orderly and impressive; and when Mr Henry Brooke MP described it as a: 'Communist-inspired mutiny' he was suffering from a rush of Tory blood to the head."

If Chuter Ede had still been at the Home Office, common sense might have prevailed. But the new Home Secretary, Sir David Maxwell Fyfe, showed no sign of preventing some local authorities from reaching at once for the heavy weaponry. Secret advice was circulated by the Association of County Councils, recommending that firefighters should be suspended from duty and evicted from fire stations by the police.

Fire chiefs were willing to put lives at risk in order to break the union. The spirit of 1945 had evaporated very fast.

United we stand: the fight for justice

But then, on 21 December, in a warehouse fire near Broad Street, London, three firefighters died – and all three were facing disciplinary charges for their part in the spit-and-polish demonstrations. They were Edward Harwood, aged 32, Leslie Skitt, 41, and Thomas Joy, 39.

A TUC official reflected: "It is deplorable that one day a person can be regarded as an enemy to our public life and the next lauded as a hero because he has shown the same determination in the execution of his duty as he had to show against an injustice."

Suddenly, victimising firefighters for refusing to scrub floors was seen clearly to be the mean and vindictive act that it was. Some fire chiefs withdrew the draconian penalties they had imposed a few weeks earlier, while in other authorities the FBU paid fines and gave financial help to men reduced in rank. The union anticipated an expensive year, and imposed a weekly levy on members.

The same month, a Conservative MP, Reader Harris, formed the Junior Fire Officers Association (JFOA) to represent sub-officers and leading firefighters. Mr Harris, a barrister and former AFS man, was already the general secretary of NAFO, the National Association of Fire Officers, and the idea of JFOA was to scoop up the officers just below the rank represented by NAFO, in the hope of weakening the FBU.

It didn't work. The London County Council would not recognise the JFOA, and that year the FBU was to report its highest membership since 1945, at 20,000. Three years later the JFOA closed, merging with NAFO: one of many failed attempts to create divisions between FBU officer members and other ranks.

FIREMEN ESCORTED OUT OF STATIONS

By HAROLD HUTCHINSON

ABOUT two-thirds of Britain's firemen yesterday carried out the first day of their token strike in support of their demand for more pay. In dozens of towns firemen were handed suspension notices, or were placed on charges of breach of discipline, but they remained in or close to their stations so that they could answer any call.

In several towns—including Exeter, Bridgwater and Cambridge—policemen politely escorted their friends the firemen from the fire stations after they had been suspended for refusing all duties except emergency and fire calls.

The firemen now get about £7 a week and were offered an extra 15s. which they refused. The Union then called on the men to refuse all routine drills and spit-and-polish duties yesterday.

The authorities decided to take action. Men were ordered to carry out their regular jobs, and when they refused were given an hour—sometimes two hours—in which to change their minds.

If They Refused

If they continued to refuse they were given typewritten suspension notices or placed on a charge of breach of discipline.

All the men had been told by the Union to stay at their posts even if suspended so that they could man the engines in case of fire.

In many cases that is what they did, but in some places where the police escorted them from the stations, they remained nearby.

Leader of the Union, Mr. John Horner, went to the House of Commons to get support from M.P.s and to protest against the suspensions.

The Union said they would bring to the notice of the T.U.C. what they called the "unprecedented tactics of intimidation" used by the local authorities.

Call to Women

Above The spit-and-polish strike for better pay was limited in its action to safeguard the public's safety. Firefighters remained in or near their stations so they could answer any calls

---

THE FBU STEPS IN

In Glasgow Central fire station, the wives of firefighters, when they came to see their husbands, had to pass the man on duty. So they often stopped to speak to him – and in June 1950 a verbal order forbade this subversive practise. The men went to the union, and the FBU sorted it out.

In February 1951 the FBU stopped Middlesex County Council from evicting Mrs Evelyn Pickworth and her five children from their home, after the death through illness of her husband, firefighter Alan Pickworth, aged 36.

Left Fire outbreak at The Old Warehouse, part of Broad Street Station Goods Depot on Eldon Street, London, 21 December 1951. FBU members Edward Harwood, Leslie Skitt and Thomas Joy all lost their lives in the blaze

Above Leading firefighter Fred Sadd was awarded the George Medal for bravery. He saved 27 lives and brought hope to countless others trapped in floods in the Yarmouth area

Facing page Whitstable, Kent, February 1953. Major flooding caused by a tidal surge forced people to leave their homes taking what they could with them

It was in this tense and confrontational atmosphere that the FBU claim went to arbitration by a panel under Sir David Ross, chairman of the Civil Service Arbitration Tribunal. Ross came down against restoring the link with police pay. A pay rise did come out of Ross's enquiry, but there was no disguising that this was a serious defeat. It left a legacy of bitterness, and it made firefighters feel undervalued.

And there were still some men whose punishment had not been reversed. Nottingham's council refused to revoke penalties, repay fines or reinstate with full seniority men who had been demoted, but the council elections in September 1952 changed a Tory majority to a hung council led by Labour, and the new council put the injustice right.

The Northern Ireland government refused even the wage increases that had been agreed. So Northern Ireland firefighters decided to continue the spit-and-polish and drill ban and threaten strike action, and in March 1953 FBU assistant general secretary Jack Grahl went to Belfast to sort it out.

Grahl persuaded the men to withdraw their proposed strike for the moment, while he talked to the police committee, who were responsible for fire brigade matters. He would demand the immediate application of English rates, failing which the men would work a 60-hour week.

So, instead of striking, the firefighters gave a new rota to the chief officer based on a 60-hour week. And they marched through Belfast. One of their slogans was:

Step by step with England
That is what they say
If it's step by step with England
What about our pay?

Grahl saw the deputy mayor (acting for the mayor, who was ill). Two hours after the meeting, the deputy mayor telephoned to say he had summoned an emergency meeting of the police committee for Monday morning, to see Grahl and his colleagues and reconsider their claim. Grahl agreed to defer the action, but warned that if the emergency meeting failed to meet the claim on

Monday, FBU members would start working a 48-hour week on Tuesday.

The politicians caved in. "The police committee agreed forthwith to British rates for firemen, leading firemen and sub-officers, promising also to meet again on Thursday to consider their application to officer grades," Grahl wrote triumphantly.

"A victory meeting was hurriedly convened at Brigade HQ. Every off-duty man attended. Never will I forget my reception as I entered to commence the meeting. The ovation, while ostensibly a tribute to me as the senior official, was, in reality, a tribute to their own unity and splendid fighting spirit…"

Grahl, an experienced and well-regarded official who had been AGS since 1946, also got stuck into the *Daily Mail* when it complained in 1953 that there were more firefighters than before the war. The reason, Grahl pointed out, was that prewar firefighters worked a 72-hour week. Did the *Mail* want to go back to that?

What price for a hero?

On 31 January 1953, a tidal surge engulfed houses on the Norfolk coast near Great Yarmouth. The 1947 Act had paved the way for firefighters to be sent to non-fire emergencies, and leading firefighter Fred Sadd, 43, of the Gorleston sub-station of Yarmouth Fire Brigade, scrambled down a 20ft embankment into the icy black water, which came up to his neck, and walked on soft mud to reach nearly 40 flooded homes whose residents were in imminent danger of drowning. Without Sadd, the death toll would have been even higher than the 300 recorded.

Newspapers lauded Sadd as a hero, and the nation gave him the George Medal. Yet the *Daily Mail* still found fault with the cost of the fire brigades. And so did the rural local authorities, though Sadd worked in a rural area. John Horner asked them: "Why must the rural ratepayer, the modern farmer with his expensive machinery and valuable crops, and the small industrial unit be fobbed off with third-rate fire protection?"

CHAPTER FOUR
A FIRE SERVICE FOR THE 1960s

No spin you can put on it can make the spit-and-polish demonstrations look like a victory. But they weren't a total defeat either.

Parity with police pay was gone for good, but the Ross Award did provide for a higher pay settlement than the employers had been willing to offer. The idea of victimising firefighters for taking action was firmly put back in its box. The Junior Fire Officers Association was never again able to sabotage FBU efforts.

Most firefighters were now in the union, and membership was rising steadily, from 15,283 in 1946 to 18,580 in 1950 and 23,810 in 1960.

And it marked a key stage in the battle to standardise wages. When Northern Ireland employers decided to opt out of the pay rise awarded by Ross in 1954, some firefighters there began a spit-and-polish demonstration again. Once again, Jack Grahl went to Belfast to sort it out.

Grahl described what happened in Belfast: "It was decided that not only would the men refuse to drill, clean etc, but would not even replenish appliances with petrol, water, hose, equipment etc after fires…" A compromise agreement gave the FBU most of what it wanted.

The demonstrations also focused attention on the jobs firefighters should never have to do. It was the beginning of the end for practices like those in Edinburgh's Lauriston fire station, where they were expected to clean the firemaster's toilet, sweep the yard, wash the balconies, launder the towels and polish the floor.

Perhaps the most insulting aspect of these jobs was that some ignorant people thought they were necessary so that the firefighters were not idle. At the start of 1957, Sir Harold Banwell, secretary of the Association of Municipal Corporations, told the annual conference of the Chief Fire Officers Association that "they must find time hanging on their hands while standing by, and productive work must be found for them".

Ted Hughes of Bournemouth replied in *Firefighter*: "The most shocking indictment of our service today… is this frantically unimaginative insistence on an endless cleaning and 'messing about' routine… Drills need not be so crude, boring and one-sided…"

"Post-war firefighters," as Shane Ewen puts it in his book *Fighting Fires*, "resented being obliged to work in pre-war conditions, but especially to undertake station duties that owed more to the Victorian tradition of servitude than the professional identity propagated by their union." *Firefighter* commented: "Personal services to officers while on duty is an infamous practice which rots the proper relations that should exist between officers and men."

Finding a voice: the drive for identity

Now fire chiefs could no longer be sure such orders would be obeyed. Firefighters were increasingly likely to refuse politely, saying it was not a proper order. Firefighter Ronald Fry of Pontypridd said just that when told to clean the boss's uniform and polish his boots. They cut his pay in half without even giving him a hearing.

The FBU took Fry's case to the Appeal Court, which agreed it was not a proper order but said Fry should have obeyed the order and then complained. But his stand was a key part of the drive for a professional identity, and a salary to match it. As improvements in the science of firefighting required better educated and trained professional firefighters, the treatment became more and more obviously insulting.

There was a much more useful way for firefighters to spend their time between calls, as John Horner pointed out in 1959 when he launched a manifesto called *A Service for the 60s*. A key document in the campaign for professionalisation, it called for firefighters to perform safety inspections and other specialist roles.

At the same time as it was fighting this battle, the union was finding its political voice. The 1951 election ushered in 13 years of Conservative rule, and that year's FBU conference decided that the union should involve itself more closely in politics.

Winston Churchill's new government was not going to do away with the welfare state, or privatise the industries that had been nationalised, or undo Ernest Bevin's settlement of the relationship between labour and capital. But it wasn't

Previous page Grays, Essex, 1950s. Many fire stations had their own control room

Facing page London, 1957. Firefighters look on as the entire front wall of a large building falls to the ground in front of them

FALLING FOUL OF THE LAW

The union's legal department didn't always win, *Firefighter* admitted in December 1957.

"It was recently engaged on behalf of one of our members whose appliance was involved in a crash with a black limousine car. The occupants of the car all gave evidence at the hearing. All five were senior police officers. We lost the case.

"One of our members in Kent got mixed up with a private car. When the doors opened, six nuns got out. We lost that case, too."

inclined to help the unions much, either. Whatever the FBU wanted for its members, it would have to fight for.

The union opposed the war in Korea, fought by the USA with British assistance from 1950 to 1953, during which the US dropped 635,000 tons of explosives on North Korea. The bombs are thought to have killed one in five of the North Korean population. We are still reaping the harvest today.

It also opposed the ruinously expensive armaments programme urged on Britain by the USA. Horner told the 1953 Trades Union Congress that its demands for more schools, more hospitals, improved social services and the rest were bled away by the rearmament drive.

In the great 1950s split in the Labour Party, the FBU stood with Nye Bevan, the founder of the National Health Service, and for unilateral nuclear disarmament.

Horner himself returned to the Labour Party after the shattering political events of 1956. That was the year that the Soviet Union invaded Hungary, and the new Soviet leader Nikita Khrushchev revealed what had long been suspected – that Stalin, who died in 1953, had been responsible for wholesale murder and torture.

The British Communist Party had claimed the allegiance of many of Horner's generation, seeming to represent a great, generous, radical creed. Now, suddenly, it looked like just another potential oppressor, and more brutal than most. A third of its members left in 1956, among them John Horner, Jack Grahl and two younger activists who were to be key figures in the union, Enoch Humphries and Terry Parry.

Grahl, aged just 44, also left the staff of the union after 10 years as assistant general secretary. Born in Leith in 1912, a year younger than Horner, he worked as a message boy, caddie, ice-cream vendor, plumber and bookseller before joining the Edinburgh AFS in 1939, swiftly becoming the city's FBU branch secretary, and then a full-time union official. He had a forceful literary style and uncompromising opinions, writing in a pamphlet, *Freedom from Fire*, just after the Second World War: "[To insurance companies] a fire now and again was always good for business. It jerked people's memories to their premium arrears."

It's not clear why he left, or what happened to him afterwards, but he played no further part in FBU affairs.

One piece of good news came out of 1956. After a long campaign, firefighters' hours were reduced from 60 to 56 a week. Five years later, the union managed to get them down to 48, though persuading each fire authority to follow this guideline was always another day's work.

The tragedies of Smithfield and Cheapside
Progress on pay was much harder. Parity with police pay had worked well, because governments – all governments, everywhere – like to look after the police. They don't feel the same about firefighters, whose pay, conditions, even safety, get forgotten except in the immediate aftermath of a big high-profile fire.

Just such a fire occurred at Smithfield meat market in London in 1958. The blaze at Union Cold Storage Company burned for three days in the centuries-old labryinth, which then collapsed. One thousand seven hundred firefighters and 389 appliances attended and more than 20 firefighters were injured.

When the first pumps arrived, thick, acrid smoke was pouring out of the maze of underground tunnels leading to cold-storage rooms. Station Officer Jack Fourt-Wells and firefighter Dick Stocking from Clerkenwell fire station headed down into the dense smoke, never to be seen alive again.

A firefighter who knew Fourt-Wells described him as "one of the old smoke eaters" who would not give up hunting for the seat of a fire. Stocking had had a brush with death four years earlier. He was sent to hospital with serious injuries after fighting a fire in a warehouse containing fruit and vegetables near London's Covent Garden, when two colleagues lost their lives.

A detailed analysis of the Smithfield fire in *Firefighter* shows that no tapes, lines or pip horns – which would warn others if a firefighter was in distress – were in use, and that both men died from carbon monoxide inhalation.

Fourt-Wells had taken his breathing apparatus off, presumably because he knew his oxygen cylinder was empty – but Stocking had his on. Yet Stocking inhaled

Facing page On 23 January 1958, firefighters fought a fire at Smithfield market for 40 hours. Station officer Jack Fourt-Wells and firefighter Dick Stocking, both of Clerkenwell fire station, lost their lives

Above In the aftermath of the Smithfield market fire, health and safety issues previously raised by the FBU, including breathing apparatus safety, were brought to the fore

Left Cheapside Street bonded warehouse fire, Glasgow, 1960. The warehouse contained more than a million gallons of whisky and rum. At the height of the blaze, 450 firefighters were involved in fighting the fire, which claimed the lives of 19 fire service personnel; 14 firefighters and five salvage corps, the highest number of fatalities in the peacetime history of the British fire service

almost as much carbon monoxide as Fourt-Wells. So something was wrong with the apparatus.

The "Proto" breathing apparatus that had failed to protect Fourt-Wells and Stocking was gradually replaced by compressed-air apparatus, though both systems remained in use for some years.

Two years later, 19 men died in a whisky warehouse in Cheapside Street, Glasgow – 14 firefighters and five men from the salvage corps. Shortly after they arrived at the fire, the warehouse exploded, blasting out the walls and showering them with tons of rubble. A fire engine was crushed and three men on it were killed before the ladder could be raised.

A huge lake of whisky and rum, a million gallons of the stuff, burned out of control for several hours. Bright-blue flames leapt 40 feet into the air, engulfing neighbouring buildings. Off-duty firefighters from Glasgow and surrounding areas rushed in to help, and 450 firefighters, 30 pumping appliances, five turntable ladders and four support vehicles attended.

Catriona Fox wrote about that night 42 years later, when firefighters were in dispute over pay: "My dad went out to work one night and never came back... My dad used to tell my mum that she would be better off financially when he was dead. Sadly, he was right...

"My older brother was a retained fireman and continued after our dad's death. Firefighters are heroes and I think that should be reflected in their wages. They deserve a good standard of living and that's why I give them my full support in the battle for a proper rate of pay."

The Glasgow fire helped trigger the Offices, Shops and Railway Premises Act 1963. This made the fire authority responsible for inspecting commercial premises. Firefighters were to carry out the inspections, as John Horner had argued that they should in 1959 in *A Service for the 60s*.

It was a far cry from the days when their chiefs thought firefighters should spend their downtime scrubbing floors and cleaning toilets.

But it left the service overstretched. Many firms avoided their obligations as long as they could. In the sixties, the union's work was at least as much about lobbying for more firefighters to be employed as about pay, conditions and safety.

The FBU told home secretary Rab Butler when they saw him in 1957: "From 1950 to 1956 fire calls, exclusive of chimney fires, nearly doubled, increasing from 63,000 to 110,000. Last year fire brigades attended in England and Wales some 226,000 calls… Yet there are fewer officers and men riding appliances today than in 1948… The union is convinced that the case is made out for a substantial increase in the number of firemen in the service …"

Horner explained to Butler: "what takes place in the first 10 minutes at a job when everyone is flat out". Butler said that local authorities wanted freedom to decide their local level of fire cover. Coming from an agricultural constituency, Butler said he knew that fire risks had multiplied because of mechanisation. But added: "I can promise you nothing."

The FBU also told Butler that women were grossly underpaid in the fire service, even though the Home Office had promised that something would be done. A *Firefighter* editorial thundered:

"If this procrastination… concerned the 20,000 firefighters and officers, there would, by now, have been a revolt in the Service. Is the government picking on the weakest section of our Service to try out their policy?… These men will not lightly stand aside and see their women colleagues treated in this manner."

But Butler turned them down, citing wage restraint. So Horner asked shadow home secretary Anthony Greenwood and Labour MP Barbara Castle to raise the issue in the House of Commons. "We know," said Castle, "that it is the government's policy to effect these economies at the expense of little groups which are unlikely to fight back . . ." They didn't get the money, but it was a marker for the future.

The Conservatives, now led by Harold Macmillan, won the 1959 election, despite (as the FBU pointed out) having vetoed the 48-hour week, resisted any manpower increase, agreed only to the barest pay increase and refused all major capital expenditure in the fire service.

Macmillan resigned in 1963, and the same year Labour leader Hugh Gaitskell died, suddenly and unexpectedly at the age of 57. So the following year it was Harold Wilson who led Labour to a narrow victory over the Conservatives led by Sir Alec Douglas-Home.

And among Labour's new MPs was the new Member for Oldbury and Halesowen, John Horner, now 53 and ready for a fresh challenge after a quarter of a century at the top of the FBU. He was replaced as general secretary by the president, Terry Parry, who beat Enoch Humphries from South Lanarkshire to the job by 2,000 votes. Humphries then replaced Parry as president.

Fight for your right: the struggle for equality

Parry, 43, was a Lancashire man who started work, aged 15, in a slate quarry. He served in the navy during the Second World War and joined the fire service in Birmingham when he was demobbed.

He quickly found himself at odds with the new Labour government. Labour, re-elected in 1966 with a bigger majority, wanted a wage freeze – just as the firefighters were about to benefit from a 7.5% pay hike Parry had negotiated. So the news that this increase was to be put on ice went down very badly with the FBU.

But the big issue of Parry's first national conference as general secretary was not pay, but hours. "The main point which really angered us was the employers' contention that firemen were not entitled to the same hours as people in industry because a fireman does not really work," he told the conference. Despite the ruling that firefighters should work a 48-hour week, many brigades were still on 56 hours.

Equal pay for women surfaced as a major union concern. Alice Prole of Essex told the conference that the union and the government were agreed on the principle, but that did not produce the money. "We don't want promises. We want the rate for the job and we want it now." Conference supported equal pay, though some delegates wolf-whistled when one of the women came to the rostrum – an early sign of the battles for equality still to be fought.

It wasn't just over firefighters' own employment that the FBU clashed with the Labour government. The relationship

Above Grays, Essex, 1960s. Breathing apparatus drill at the fire station

was less friendly than it had been in the Attlee years. Harold Wilson refused US president Lyndon Johnson's insistent and impatient demands that Britain should send troops to fight in Vietnam. But the FBU wanted him to go further – to condemn the use of ferocious new weapons, including napalm, which, when ignited, sticks to practically anything and burns for up to 10 minutes. The effects of napalm on the human body are unbearably painful and almost always cause death.

A 1969 White Paper on trade union reform produced by Wilson's employment minister, the FBU's old friend Barbara Castle, and called *In Place of Strife*, advocated restrictions on the unions' current rights. The FBU joined with the rest of the trade unions in condemning it.

That was also the year in which the FBU came right to the heart of the trade union movement, its general secretary for the first time winning a place on the TUC General Council.

Discontent and despair: rumblings begin

The FBU view of the government was summed up by president Enoch Humphries, who also became president of the Scottish TUC in 1968. He said that on the: "litmus test issues" – unemployment, the health service, social services – the Labour government: "ran for cover into the bosom of the orthodox Treasury."

There were, of course, Labour MPs who agreed with Humphries. One of these was John Horner. Surprisingly not offered a post in the government, probably because of his Communist past, he was a persistent if polite critic from the back benches.

"It was a great pity," wrote Labour MP Tam Dalyell later, "that Horner was not brought into the leadership of the government at the time. Had he been there I believe that the relationship between party and parliamentary party would have been such that victory in 1970 would have been possible."

Horner put some of the knowledge and understanding that had so impressed Dalyell into a book, *Studies in Industrial Democracy*, published in 1974.

Horner remains the key figure in FBU history, whose career at crucial moments, especially in 1938 when he took on the union's leadership and won at the age of just 27, demonstrates a certainty and a will that few possess. Yet those who knew him talk of someone very different: a scholar, a polymath, fascinated by art, philosophy and English literature.

He lost his seat in 1970, one of the Labour casualties of Edward Heath's Conservative general election victory, and went cheerfully into retirement.

By then, the discontent in the fire stations was tangible. The government had failed to provide an effective way of setting pay ever since the end of police comparability in 1952.

And in the seventies there was a further calamitous decline in pay. In 1971, firefighters earned £2.58 more than the average wage. By 1977 their pay of £65.70 per week was £12.90 behind average male earnings. Frustration after a quarter of a century of broken promises was about to explode.

DUDGEONS WHARF FIRE 17 JULY 1969

The funeral of five firefighters killed at Dudgeons Wharf, a disused oil storage depot in East London. It is thought a spark from cutting equipment, combined with flammable vapours inside the oil tanks, led to a fatal explosion. Michael Gamble and Alfred Smee (Millwall fire station), John Appleby and Terrance Breen (Brunswick Road fire station), and Paul Carvosso (Cannon Street fire station) were killed from the resulting blast. Their funeral service was held at All Saints Church in Stratford before the cortege moved off to the City of London Crematorium. Also killed that day was Richard Adams, a construction worker.

As a result of this incident, the Hazchem Code was introduced in the 1970s. All buildings, vehicles and storage areas containing hazardous chemicals must have a coded sign that informs firefighters of the immediate steps they must take to protect themselves and the public if these areas are involved in a fire.

Facing page Anti-Vietnam vigil outside the US embassy, 1973, with FBU general secretary (and former president) Terry Parry, looking directly at the camera

CHAPTER FIVE

THE FIRST NATIONAL FIREFIGHTERS' STRIKE

By 1977, firefighters' wages had been reduced to about three quarters of the average male earnings. Many firefighters were forced to take second jobs or seek social security benefits.

They felt not only that they deserved their claim to the average wage plus 10% for the dangers they faced and the skills they needed, but that they had been promised it. The 1970 Holroyd Report had said that pay should be comparable with the "national average earnings of skilled craftsmen".

But successive governments' pay policies – first Heath's Conservative government, then Wilson's Labour government – meant the recommendation had never been implemented.

Ministers' priority was bringing down inflation, which hovered around 25% in 1975, and 16% for the next two years. Prime minister James Callaghan and chancellor Denis Healey wanted trade-union support to keep wages down. They instigated a voluntary incomes policy.

What could be done? For many firefighters, the inspiration was what had been done in Glasgow in 1973. The Glasgow fire service had been finding it hard to recruit firefighters – it was 23% short of its authorised establishment and getting by on huge amounts of overtime.

Morale was low, and the previous year a huge fire in a cash-and-carry warehouse in Kilbirnie Street selling textiles, clothing and household goods had claimed the lives of seven Glasgow firefighters.

Firefighter James Rook was trapped in a flareup of the fire in an attic. The second expedition to rescue him, led by divisional officer Andrew Quinn, found Rook and dug him out of the collapsed stock. But as they were dragging him away, a fast, fierce eruption of heat and flame across the first-floor ceiling engulfed the rescuers, and the structure collapsed on them.

A roll call in the street showed who was missing, and further rescue attempts were made from ladders through the first-floor windows. When it was clear that no survivors were to be found – Quinn and his men were all dead – rescuers were ordered to withdraw from the building until the fire was under control. They attacked the fire externally, using equipment including turntable ladders and hydraulic platforms.

For taking that sort of risk, why should firefighters be paid so little that they had to claim free school meals? And why should they be starved of people and resources?

An unofficial strike in the city the following year, from 26 October to 5 November 1973, led to them getting an extra £2.48 a week above what was negotiated nationally.

If it worked in Glasgow, why not in the whole country? But FBU general secretary Terry Parry supported the TUC line, telling the union's 1976 annual conference: "We are not propping up capitalism, but seeking to preserve the economy of Britain…"

Callaghan and Healey insisted that they could not make a special case for the fire service. They believed private-sector employers, who were under pressure to increase pay, would complain bitterly if ministers breached their own rules for the public sector.

A working party chaired by Lord McCarthy recommended that the best comparison for assessing firefighters' wages was "the generality of jobs in the community". The FBU made a claim based on this, which would have broken through the 10% limit. It also sought to reduce the working week to 42 hours, and to add 10% to account for the danger and skills involved in the job.

PARRY CHALLENGES PAY POLICY

TUC representatives meeting prime minister James Callaghan and chancellor Denis Healey to discuss pay policy routinely included general council member Terry Parry, who became TUC president in October 1979.

"The government seems to be relying on its expressed faith that the extra spending power provided through cuts in income tax (which does not affect the low-paid anyway) is somehow going to generate industry and create jobs to absorb those who have lost jobs from cuts in public expenditure," he said.

"I don't know if the government really believes this will happen, but I don't."

Above Kilbirnie Street fire, Glasgow, 1972. Seven firefighters died, the second major fire service tragedy in 12 years after the Cheapside Street disaster in 1960

Previous page Blackpool, 1977. Firefighters on national strike for more pay protest against Labour Prime Minister Jim Callaghan

Facing page An unofficial walkout in 1973 by Glasgow firefighters was the first full-scale withdrawal of labour in the union's history. Here, James Flockhart, leader of the Glasgow firefighters strike committee, arrives with other delegates to a noisy welcome at a special FBU national conference in London

Above *Daily Mirror*,
7 November 1977.
Firefighters vote for stoppage
by an overwhelming majority
of 25,000 to 13,000. The
army was put on standby
in case of strike

Right Firefighters in the West
Midlands, 1977, on the first
firefighters national strike for
a pay increase of 30%

In total, the claim was worth around 30% – against a government incomes policy of 10%.

The 1977 FBU conference in May demanded a real increase – not just an increase for inflation – as well as a 40-hour week. Home secretary Merlyn Rees replied: "We cannot opt out of the problem of the economy of the country and the economy of the world."

In this atmosphere, the meeting a week later between Rees and the FBU looked doomed. And it was. Parry tried hard to get Rees to give him something he could take to his members. But ministers feared that any settlement the firefighters might accept would open the floodgates for a million low-paid local authority workers.

Meanwhile the pressure for a strike was building. Twenty Liverpool firefighters were dismissed after an "emergency cover only" strike, and reinstated only after the dismissals provoked further action. Calls for the executive to ballot for strike action came from the West Midlands, Greater Manchester, Lancashire and Strathclyde.

At a Recall conference on 7 November 1977 in Eastbourne, Parry asked the 300 delegates for four more weeks for negotiations.

He didn't get it. Instead, the conference agreed this motion, proposed by Ronnie Scott, who later became the union's president for most of the 1990s:

"The conference agrees to commence strike action as from the day-shift Monday, 14 November 1977, in support of a wage claim based on average earnings plus 10%… strike action to be terminated upon the attainment of this claim or the decision of a Recall conference."

Terry Parry had tried desperately to avoid this. According to historian John Saville, Parry "argued to the last that a national strike did not represent the will of the majority of the membership but was the policy of a minority of militants of the left. He was wrong."

But once the decision was taken, writes Saville, Parry "used his considerable capacities to support the strike, to keep the union together, and to continue to press for negotiations which would satisfy his members." A reluctant strike leader he may have been, but he also turned into a committed and effective one.

A big man with an effective platform style, Parry had a precious ability to deflect criticism with humour. His jokes were not always very good – there was one about a cross-eyed javelin thrower who didn't win many medals but kept the crowd on its toes – but they were part of the folklore that surrounded him.

Push comes to shove: the strike of '77

Furious newspaper editorials condemned the strike decision. "Have a heart," screamed a *Daily Express* headline. But they did not succeed in making the public hostile. Opinion polls showed majority support for making the firefighters a special case.

Scotland Yard warned that the Provisional IRA might choose the time of a strike to plant bombs. Merlyn Rees ramped up the pressure in a broadcast on the eve of the strike: "I cannot believe that they would allow children's or old people's homes to burn down around their occupants."

But firefighters knew better than anyone the sort of dangers that the nation faced. Liverpool's Ronald Sherbern probably spoke for many others when he told the *Daily Telegraph*: "We don't want to strike. It makes us sick to do it, but what other choice have we got?"

On the evening of 14 November 1977, more than 30,000 FBU members were on strike.

NORTHERN IRELAND: SERVING ALL COMMUNITIES

In the mid-1970s, FBU officials secretly met paramilitary leaders on both sides of the Northern Ireland conflict. They made it clear that firefighters were there to serve all members of the community regardless of political divisions.

"We were very reluctant to fortify ourselves or fortify fire stations, because it was important to us to be seen not to be part of anything to do with the security forces," says firefighter Harry Welsh.

"We were doing the same job as firefighters anywhere, plus we had this other stuff to deal with and we were getting less money. So when the firefighters' strike took place in 1977, firefighters here had had enough. That's why there was such support for the strike."

Feelings were high. Sub-officer Michael Brown, in charge of the Windsor fire station, was widely reported when he said: "We will not turn out even if the Queen is trapped in Windsor Castle."

Alan McLean was 18 and followed his father into the fire service in Tyne and Wear 10 months before the strike began.

"I was a young single man living at my parents' house and didn't recognise the impoverished way the firefighters on my shift were living. I found out that some of their children were on free school meals," he says.

"Their peers – in shipbuilding, heavy industry, big factories – were on much better money.

"The push for a strike was coming up from the rank and file. Members got so angry about pay and conditions. There were a lot of angry young men. They were different from the people who joined after the war, who were looking for pension and job security."

For Alan, it was the start of a lifetime's union activism, and he was FBU president from 2011 until early 2018. Picket lines were set up all over the country. John Horner, by then a distinguished retired politician of 66, walked past Soho fire station:

"A lone fireman stood warming himself over his brazier, a clipboard in his hand, soliciting signatures from passers-by in support of the union. I signed the sheet and moved inside. My name meant nothing to him. I said absently, yet hoping to strike up a conversation: 'I don't think I have been in this appliance room since the night the bomb fell.'

"He looked at me. 'What bomb?' he asked. He was very young. And I knew then that I was getting very old."

Ministers called in troops, and the FBU instructed its members not to interfere with them. But pickets should seek to dissuade everyone except servicemen from trying to do firefighters' work.

The National Association of Fire Officers (NAFO), said its members would not cross picket lines. In the event, though, many of their members did work with military firefighters, and the Chief and Assistant Chief Fire Officers Association said it would cross lines.

The army had outdated equipment and only a few hours' training. They had no training for dealing with fires in high-rise blocks, and were not qualified to use the fire brigades' engines (which were behind picket lines, anyway.) So they relied on more than 1,000 engines dating from the 1950s – the Green Goddesses.

More than once during the strike, firefighters left their picket lines to help out in dangerous situations. One group of pickets, still wearing their uniforms and pickets' armbands, rushed to the scene of a fire at St Andrew's Hospital in Bow, East London, after a basement storeroom caught light.

"We couldn't let them die. For God's sake, it was a hospital, what else could we do but come and help?" said one of the officers, while a firefighter, Barry Holmes, added: "The situation here was really dangerous and people could have died if we had not come."

While opinion polls showed more than 60% public support for the firefighters, the establishment seemed to be ganging up against them. The Catholic Archbishop of Westminster, Cardinal Basil Hume, wrote in the *Times*: "Christians… are dismayed that the lives of innocent individuals are put at risk in… a struggle for economic benefits…"

In November, 10,000 firefighters and their families came to a rally in Hyde Park and handed in a petition to Downing Street with half a million signatures.

Prime minister Jim Callaghan met the FBU executive and told them: "Your strike… cannot be allowed to succeed." He offered to ensure the government underwrote any future pay formula.

But this wasn't good enough. The FBU asked the TUC for backing for a campaign against pay restraint. The TUC said no.

Three weeks into the strike, in December, the employers proposed that the firefighters' weekly wage would in future be linked to that of the average of skilled workers, with a reduction in working hours. But the immediate rise must be in line with government policy, at only 10%, in two stages – in November 1978 and again in 1979. Parity with other skilled workers would not come for two years.

It wasn't enough. FBU leaders made one more effort to persuade the TUC to campaign against pay restraint.

It failed. More than 800 firefighters jeered at the TUC response when Terry Parry came out of the meeting and reported this.

The failure to win TUC support was a blow to the campaign and increased pressure on the union for a settlement. FBU negotiators sought improvements to the employers' offer.

This included a pay formula for the future. It would tie firefighters' pay to the top quarter of male manual workers' earnings. And it would be guaranteed against any future government incomes policy. The working week would come down to 42 hours by 1 April 1979.

But the 10% limit would hold, for the present.

This, the executive decided, was sufficient to justify a Recall conference, which was held on 12 January 1978 in Bridlington.

Many firefighters were very short of money after nine weeks without pay. They felt undermined by NAFO's help for the military firefighters, by part-time firefighters who were not union members, and by the TUC's decision to abide by the government's pay policy.

So they voted by three to one to go back to work. It felt like a defeat. There was huge bitterness. But the link established between firefighters' pay and other manual workers' earnings paid off in the long run.

The 42-hour week was also a victory, though there was still to be a battle over how it was to work.

By August *Firefighter* was condemning employers: "trying to use the 42 hour week to cut standards of fire cover". "Don't play with fire" read a placard on a local demonstration.

But, region by region, the 42-hour week came in by agreement. South Yorkshire was first, on 23 December 1978, and the rest of the country was rushing to meet the deadline of 1 April 1979.

"In the next two years," says one former firefighter, "we got pretty well everything. Personally, my conditions got better with a substantial increase in pay and a reduction of the working week."

The pay formula, with its guaranteed pay rises, lasted for the next 25 years.

'Okay, you lads that broke the strike, let's let bygones be bygones—come on down and shake hands.'

Above Cartoon showing firefighters' feelings towards strike breakers after returning to work. Some refused to work with 'blacklegs'

Facing page Merseyside firefighters, December 1977, picketing their station weeks into the national pay strikes

A WOMAN'S PLACE

In the summer of 1979, Marion Gaunt of Lincolnshire became the first woman on the union's executive committee since the Second World War, as well as the first ever representative for control staff.

She told *Firefighter*: "I was shocked to discover, on joining the union in 1956, that control staff were badly organised within it. Overtime without pay was being worked and discretionary benefits were denied to us. We appeared to be second class citizens in the fire service." She played a key role in organising the control staff section of the FBU.

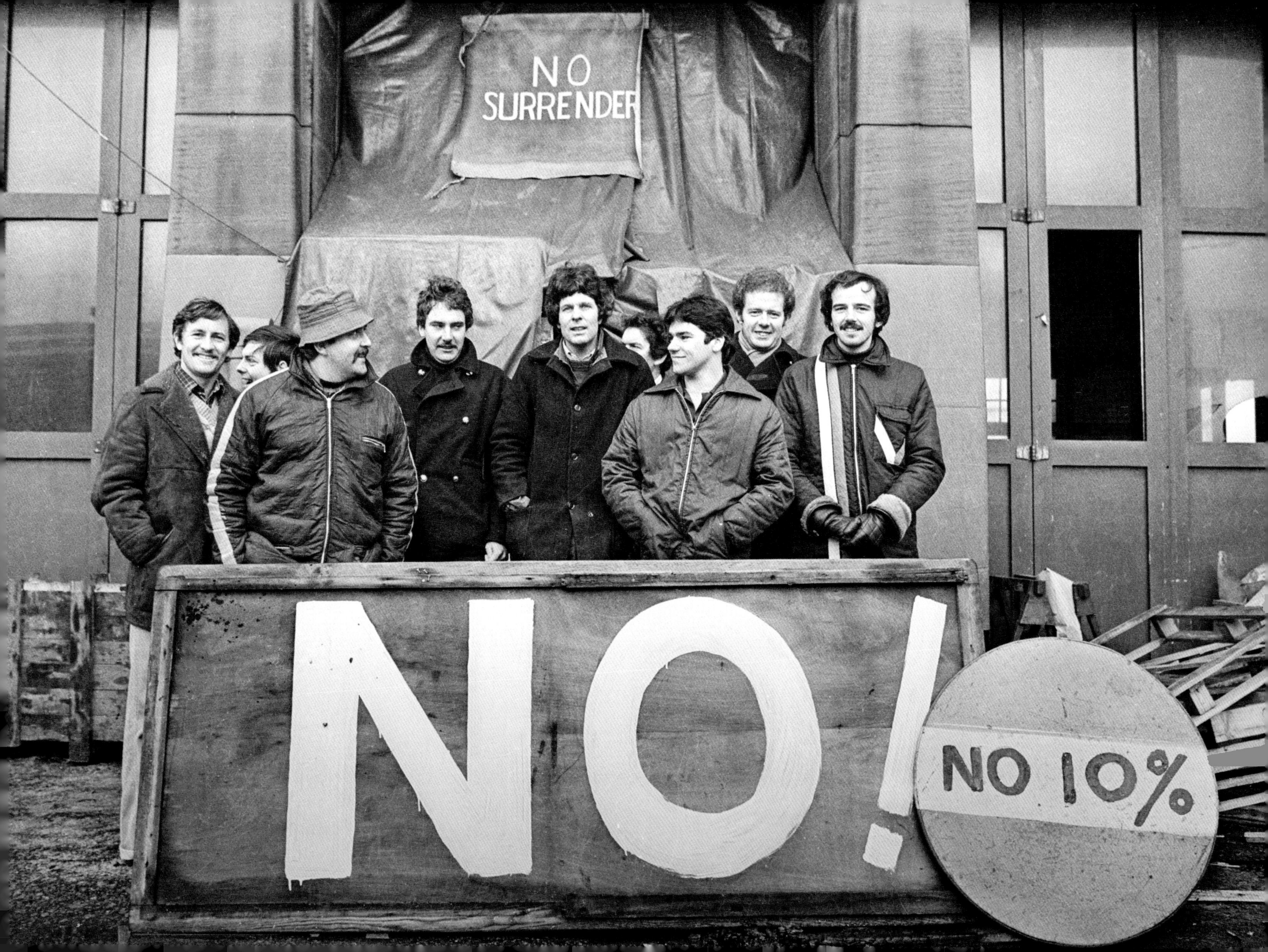
NO
SURRENDER
NO!
NO 10%

CHAPTER SIX
FROM THATCHER TO THE TWIN TOWERS

n 1979 Mike Fordham, 28, became the youngest national officer in the union's history after John Horner. Fordham came from a fire service family, as far back as his great-grandfather, a firefighter at the turn of the century.

Within days of his election, 10 people were killed from the fumes of plastic furniture stuffing – polyurethane – in a fire at the Woolworths store in Manchester. Fordham played a key role in the subsequent campaign to make furniture safe.

Firefighters arrived to find smoke billowing from the six-storey building and people calling for help from the windows. They fought the blaze for two-and-a-half hours, helping people out of the building via doors, windows and the roof.

Just one year later, five children died in a Sunderland house fire from the same deadly substance.

Polyurethane also contributed to the death of firefighter Stephen Maynard of Poplar fire station in January 1980. An aluminium tank was being cut out of a ship docked in the Regent's Canal when sparks lit up the tank's polyurethane coating.

Maynard, 27, went into the hold. As the heat rose, the firefighters there were ordered to leave. Three men got to the top of the scorching ladder in time, but the fourth, Stephen, did not make it. He fell, smashing his breathing apparatus, as the tank burst into flames.

For Fordham, it all revived a disturbing memory. On Christmas Day 1968, aged 18, his first Christmas in the fire service, he carried five dead children out of a fire. "They died because of a foam settee in their house," he said. "Mum and dad managed to escape, all five children died.

"Every firefighter knew the dangers of foam furniture, but we kept going to fires where one person died, two people died, a couple of children died, a couple of old people died. To us, that was horrific, but government didn't give a damn. They probably didn't even know."

Fordham calculated that 100 people were being killed by this substance every year. "Once most modern furniture caught fire, people had a maximum of two minutes to get out before the fumes overcame them," he wrote.

"The British public are now in an impossible position. Either they buy foam furniture, which they know to be a hazard, or they sit on the floor. The only other furniture that the manufacturers have made available is out of the price range of the working man."

But this was a difficult time to demand stronger regulations. The Labour government fell in 1979 to be replaced by Margaret Thatcher's Conservative government, which thought of regulation only as a burden on business. Furniture manufacturers lobbied ministers against further regulation.

But at Christmas 1987, 20 children died in different fires. A powerful FBU response, supported by the Chief Officers' Association and Ian McCartney MP, brought about regulations forcing manufacturers to make furniture fillings and covers from safer materials.

"We didn't have a Christmas that year, those that were running the campaign," says Fordham. "We spent seven days a week, 24 hours a day, running that campaign over that Christmas to try and get government to change their mind. It wouldn't have happened without the FBU.

"I think one of the things the FBU should be proudest of is what we've done on public safety. We've tried to crystal-ball gaze whereas government tends to do stable-door legislation."

Change at the top: same old battles

Terry Parry, who had been in poor health, retired in 1981 – he died the following April, aged only 61. "He will certainly not be remembered for his lousy jokes," Greg Bluestone of the London Fire Brigade told Parry's last conference. But "the fact that we as a union are financially sound is almost entirely due to him."

Parry told the conference: "My old man used to say: he's the one who's never been to work; he's been a sailor, a fireman and a trade union official."

He added: "What this Thatcher government is doing is rapidly destroying all the things that were achieved."

Increasingly, in the Parry years, firefighters were treated and paid as skilled professionals. That, and preventing Thatcher from destroying the fire service and other public

RHYME OF THE TIMES

In 1981, one of the late 20th century's best known humorous poets, Roger Woddis, wrote a poem for *Firefighter*. It's the story of a doctor who takes private patients. When his house catches fire, he calls the fire brigade:

He heard the operator's voice:
"You realise you have a choice –
The public service, free to all,
With firemen tramping through the hall
And axes hacking at the stair
And water, water everywhere;
But as your case is not unique
They may not come til Thursday week."

Alas, the frantic Dr Fell
Could only splutter: "What the hell –"
Before the girl, in accents bland,
Informed him: "On the other hand
We have a private system too
Which means you needn't join the queue."
The doctor failed to see the joke
And watched his house go up in smoke.

Previous page The FBU played a crucial part in securing new fire safety regulations after the devastating 1987 King's Cross station fire which killed 31 people including Station Officer Colin Townsley

Facing page The union was involved in a campaign which led to The Furniture and Furnishings (Fire Safety) Regulations 1988 following the 1979 Manchester Woolworths fire

Above Bombing of the Conservative Party conference at the Grand Hotel, Brighton, 1984

Facing page The funeral of station officer Colin Townsley of Soho fire station, one of the first firefighters at the scene of the King's Cross fire

services, were, for the next two decades, to be the two main preoccupations of the new general secretary, 40-year-old Ken Cameron.

Born in the Highlands of Scotland, Cameron started to train for the police, then became a trainee reporter on the *Aberdeen Press and Journal*.

Along with an interest in betting on horses, he liked to tell stories of his brief and less than glorious journalistic career. While covering the Highland Games, he listed the girl who won the egg-and-spoon race as having won the caber toss. Covering a swimming competition, he fell into the pool. Word got back to Cameron's editor, who fired him.

He moved to Birmingham, joined the fire brigade, and with his life-long passion for social justice soon became active in the FBU. During the 1977-78 strike he was a member of the executive council.

A popular and convivial figure in the trade union movement, he followed Parry onto the general council of the TUC.

"There is no doubt," he wrote in 1983, "that the intention of the Tories, should they win the next election, is to bring in legislation to take away the right to strike in essential services such as the fire service."

The Tories did win the 1983 general election, by a landslide. FBU disappointment was only slightly lessened by the victory of one of their own, executive member Terry Fields, who became the MP for Broadgreen in Liverpool.

The next year, the Provisional IRA planted a bomb in Brighton's Grand Hotel during the Conservative party conference. Firefighters rescued several senior Tory politicians.

Margaret Thatcher wrote to the East Sussex Brigade chief officer praising "the speed of response, the skill of operation and, above all, the magnificent courage of members of the fire service in working in conditions of great and growing danger... I am writing to ask you to pass on my personal appreciation to all those involved for their devoted and selfless professionalism to which some of my closest friends owe their lives..."

"I think the Tories took their guns away from us because of the Brighton bomb," says Alan McLean. But the government did seek confrontation with the National Union of Mineworkers.

In September 1984, Ken Cameron asked the TUC to help the beleaguered miners in the great 1984-85 miners' strike: "The National Union of Mineworkers (NUM) received the backing they sought at this year's TUC. Now it is up to the movement as a whole to respond."

Soon afterwards, Cameron took a call from Arthur Scargill. The miners' president said he needed £200,000 in cash as a loan.

The FBU had donated money already. Cameron said that to loan such a large sum of money he needed authorisation from his executive, which was not due to meet for another month. Scargill told him that unless Cameron could give him the cash that morning, he could not pay his staff.

Cameron decided to give Scargill the money and clear it with his executive later. He met Scargill's driver Jim Parker at the bank.

The money would not fit into Cameron's briefcase, so they found some cardboard boxes which had once held packets of crisps. The bank manager asked what Cameron wanted the money for. Cameron said: "Where's the nearest bookie?"

As they drove away, Parker said: "He's odd, that bank manager." Cameron replied: "He's stupid. He didn't ask the name of the horse."

After the strike the money was repaid.

Bradford fire: FBU calls for change

Four months after the miners were forced back to work, the FBU conference, in Bridlington on 15-17 May 1985, was overshadowed by the Bradford City stadium fire, just four days before the conference began.

The fire, at the Football League third division fixture between Bradford City and Lincoln City, killed 56 people and injured at least 265.

Bradford's Valley Parade stadium was known for its antiquated design and facilities. Warnings had been given about a build-up of litter just below the seats.

The stand's wooden roof, covered with layers of highly flammable roofing felt, offered no resistance to the fire.

In less than four minutes the entire stand was in flames.

Burning timbers and molten materials fell from the roof onto the crowd below. Black smoke enveloped a passageway behind the stand, where many spectators were trying to escape.

The FBU's evidence to the resulting public inquiry helped pave the way for new safety standards in football grounds.

Battle lines drawn: 1980s conflict

The next year brought a ferocious battle between the print unions and Rupert Murdoch's News International newspaper empire. Cameron was prominent among the print unions' supporters, so much so that he became a target for the Special Branch. Undercover officers spied on the FBU, and Cameron featured in a 215-page file on trade unionists' activities.

One really bad government idea was apparently stifled at birth. The Adam Smith Institute proposed what amounted to a return to the Victorian system of fire cover: "It is possible to envisage the operation of totally private fire brigades providing protection on a subscription basis."

Such a system would certainly have ensured that many more people died in the King's Cross fire of 1987.

The fire started under a wooden escalator serving the Piccadilly line, erupted into the underground ticket hall and killed 31 people. One of the first firefighters on the scene, station officer Colin Townsley of Soho fire station, was killed.

A public inquiry came up with 157 recommendations. The FBU contributed to these, but complained that, as usual, this was shutting the stable door after the horse had bolted. It said that the Channel Tunnel, then under construction, risked another King's Cross, only far, far worse.

Mike Fordham believes union pressure was critical here: "Some of the safety aspects of the Channel Tunnel are there today because of the FBU."

The King's Cross fire was followed by a 1988 train crash at Clapham Junction in which 35 people were killed and 484 injured, and another at Purley Station in 1989 which killed five people and injured 88.

And after all that, London's chief fire officer wanted to close six fire stations and lose 23 appliances and between 500-700 jobs.

Union officials thought it madness, and said so. They won that battle. By April 1990 Ken Cameron was able to report: "Jobs have been saved and the public will be better protected as a result of common sense prevailing in the London brigade."

As if to underline the foolishness of cuts, two London firefighters lost their lives the next year in an operation that went disastrously wrong.

Terry Hunt, 33, and David Stokoe, 25, died after running out of air while fighting a fire in breathing apparatus in Hays Business Services' warehouse in Bromley-by-Bow. The fire was started by arsonists.

Both men were from Silvertown fire station, where the 28-year-old North East London FBU area secretary, Matt Wrack, had worked before moving to Kingsland station in Hackney.

"I got home from work and there was a call from the regional office saying, 'We think we've lost someone,'" Wrack recalls. "I went to the scene. There were 100 firefighters there. I started to do interviews, I met the affected watches, met the families, went to the inquest and I wrote the report with Jim Fitzpatrick. It made me think about how we interact with bereaved families as a union. I thought the union needed to do more. A death at work has a massive impact on the workforce."

He wrote in *Firefighter*: "Such a tragedy hits us all very hard, the Green Watch at Silvertown Fire Station, others who knew and worked with David and Terry."

The report by Wrack and Fitzpatrick identified errors in procedure. It also pointed out that there was a policy at the warehouse to delay calling the brigade by contacting the company monitoring the fire alarm. The material stored included sensitive documentation concerning fraud, liquidations and receiverships.

Safety was a big issue in the Thatcher years, but pay seemed to have been put to bed. The FBU was able to keep the pay settlement reached at the end of the 1977 strike. This provided regular annual pay rises on an agreed formula.

Above FBU President Bill Deal leads a union rally in Norwich against cuts to the fire service, 1979

Facing page The 1988 Clapham Junction train crash in which 35 people were killed and nearly 500 injured

SAFETY OR PROFIT?

The railways, nationalised by the Attlee government in 1948, were privatised in the Thatcher years. Labour came to power in 1997 and pledged to take them back into public ownership – but it didn't.

In 1999, 31 people died in a horrific rail crash in Paddington. Ken Cameron pointed out that the inquiry into the 1997 Southall crash, in which seven people died, was still sitting. The recommendations on safety following 35 deaths in the Clapham crash of 1988 had not been fully implemented.

Profit, not safety, was the priority, said Cameron, and it was time for the Labour government to fulfil its pledge.

When the government thought about attacking it, Cameron was quick to defend it forcefully:

"Publicly, the government has been unstinting in its praise for the work of the emergency services like the fire service… But the true face of the government is now revealed in an attempt to destroy the fire service's joint bargaining arrangements . . . The national pay formula is under attack, the formula won through national strike action."

But by 1992 the formula was starting to look less attractive. That year it produced a 5.6% rise. Cameron was uneasily aware that some members felt it wasn't enough, and were starting to question the value of the formula.

He felt sure they would be worse off without it. It came out of "our first and only national strike," he said. Before the strike, "firefighters were low paid." The formula was the strike's big long-term gain.

Cameron's determination to hang onto the formula must have been hardened by the unexpected general election result of 1992.

The Tories were re-elected. It meant, said Cameron, "a continuation of the Tories' policy of misery for the unemployed, the homeless, those living in the poverty trap, and the starvation of funds from our health, education and social services".

The next year, the government said it would only fund pay rises to a maximum of 1.5%. Any more would have to come from local authorities – and they refused to confirm that they would pay.

That year's FBU conference in Bridlington authorised strike action if necessary, to defend the formula.

At the eleventh hour, the employers agreed to fund the settlement in full – but there was a catch. They wanted to save money by not implementing it straight away. "If the formula produces more than 1.5% at November 1993 we will have to suspend its full operation for 12 months" they said. In the event, the formula produced just 1.4%, which was therefore paid at once.

At once, furious right-wing commentators began to search for ways to prevent the union exercising this kind of influence. There was a campaign for strikes in essential services to be made illegal.

Andrew Roberts wrote in the *Times*: "It is time to warn the Conservative Party of the consequences of a return to the craven stance which their liberal wing has adopted towards organised labour since the war . . . The absurd goal of full employment came to be accepted by Tories as being worthwhile in itself, rather than a temporary by-product of an over-revved economy."

The return of firefighting women

By the 1980s, full employment, whether "absurd" or not, included women. The decade brought Britain's first peacetime frontline women firefighters. The very first, in 1982, was London's Sue Batten. Aged 30, she handled the media furore, and the inevitable stupid questions, with quiet dignity.

With a move from London to Avon in 1993, she did the job for 25 years, and when she retired, Sian Griffiths, chair of the FBU London women's committee, wrote in *Siren*, an FBU magazine for women firefighters:

"Sue's ambition was only to become a firefighter, not to be the first woman. Sue, who is a remarkable but modest woman, remained a firefighter for her entire career and has, whether she likes it or not, become a legend in her lifetime. She continued to stay in touch with the women of the LFB and was a stalwart in her support of other women."

The Greater London Council encouraged women firefighters in the 1980s, with special pre-entry courses. By 1990 there were 34 women firefighters in the London Fire Brigade.

1996 marked a tragic milestone: the first peacetime woman firefighter to die in a fire. Avon firefighter Fleur Lombard, 21, was called out to a fire that destroyed a supermarket in Staple Hill, Bristol. It had been started deliberately by a security guard.

Lombard was caught in a flashover and killed by intense heat. Her body was found just a few yards from the exit.

Two years earlier she had received the silver axe award as the outstanding recruit in her training school. She was one of only eight women among Avon's 700 firefighters.

Even then, not everyone in the fire service was ready to accept frontline women firefighters as equals. The year

BOMB BLAST TAKES OUT STATION

On 31 July 1989 the Royal Courts of Justice building directly opposite Belfast's Central fire station in Chichester Street was attacked.

A huge bomb concealed in a van was driven up to the front of the building. The alarm was raised and fire crews had to abandon the station and all the fire engines and escape by means of a rear door. Army bomb disposal officers arrived at the scene and deployed a robot device to approach the van. As it approached, the bomb exploded, blasting the robot across the road and through the first-floor window of the fire station causing significant damage.

The burning fuel tank of the van was blown into the FBU office, above the fire station, destroying the union archives. The fire station was so badly damaged that it could no longer be used and arrangements had to be made to accommodate fire crews and bring spare fire engines into use at other stations until repairs could be made.

Facing page London, 1982. Sue Batten, the UK's first woman frontline firefighter in peacetime

BLAINA 1996

A summer 1995 picture of the Blaina Fire Station crew. Stephen Griffin (left back row) and Kevin Lane (front row right) died after going back into a burning house in search of a trapped child. As a result of the fire, breathing apparatus procedures were revised and the union recommended that all firefighters must receive basic and continuation training using real fire training techniques and procedures.

Left Firefighters douse a blazing car after a riot erupted at an anti-poll tax demonstration, The Strand, London, 1990

after Lombard died, the employment appeal tribunal found in favour of FBU member Tania Clayton, who had suffered 10 years of demeaning treatment and was fully backed by the FBU.

She was made to get up early to serve tea and coffee in bed for male officers, and given extra drills and training. They made her spend an hour on a turntable ladder being spun around.

The tribunal declared that Hereford and Worcester Fire Service and two named officers should bear: "individual and collective shame. Discriminatory attitudes were so rife, managerial control so little and attitudes so hardened that it is no wonder it took place, with management completely unable to deal with it."

Ken Cameron said: "I hope this will kick-start chief fire officers into at least taking equal opportunities as seriously as the union does."

Some of the union's own members still had to be convinced, and a new national officer, Andy Gilchrist, wrote in *Firefighter* that pornography should not be taken into fire stations:

"Taking explicit sexual material into the workplace is not acceptable, just as it is not acceptable to take racist or sectarian literature or memorabilia into work… Pornography can project an image of women as passive, physical objects whose primary function is to fulfil the sexual fantasies of men."

New Labour, old problems
Tania Clayton left the fire service in 1994. That year, Labour leader John Smith died suddenly, of a heart attack. Smith had been coasting to victory at the next election, as the Conservative party imploded.

His successor Tony Blair seemed like a very new sort of Labour leader. Though the union continued to call for a Labour government, it was not at all sure it liked what it was seeing.

For the first time since the 1920s, the union's affiliation to Labour came under serious question.

In October 1996 Ken Cameron wrote in *Firefighter*: "This year's TUC… was overshadowed by statements from Labour party spokespersons on the continuing relationship between the party and the trade union movement…David Blunkett, when decrying strikes in the public sector, stated: 'An incoming Labour government is not going to tolerate the activities of armchair revolutionaries whose only interest is disruption and who see disputes as a means of mischief making.'

"I find such statements objectionable. It is an insult to our members in Merseyside or Derbyshire who have taken action, not out of greed or self-interest, but to save our service from destruction."

Pre-millenium tensions: national strike averted
As it became clear that New Labour wanted to shackle the unions and limit employment rights, Cameron said: "We can no longer rely on them to be our natural allies."

All the same, after Labour's landslide victory in 1997, he tried hard to be positive. He and the new home secretary, Jack Straw, agreed on an independent investigation into equality in the fire service.

It found institutional racism and sexism. Cameron responded by supporting the creation of black and ethnic minority, women's and, eventually, gay and lesbian sections within the union.

But this collaboration could not disguise the underlying tensions. Cameron wrote, with masterly understatement: "Whilst we are conscious that they cannot undo the damage wreaked on working people for 18 years overnight, maintaining the Tories' public spending limits is a mistake."

There were several local strikes against local cuts.

And eventually but inevitably, the hard-won pay formula came under threat. In March 1999 came a proposal to break up the National Joint Council (NJC) and leave everything to local negotiation.

Within two months, Cameron was talking seriously about national strike action. "We have exhausted all other alternatives… I believe that a national strike is the only realistic option left to us."

The next month, June, he wrote: "We are perilously close to the second national strike in the UK fire service."

Above Fleur Lombard, who died fighting a supermarket fire in Bristol, February 1996. She was the first woman firefighter to die on duty in peacetime

75

Flame
STRIKE!
FOR
THE PAY
FORMUL
Flame
STRIKE!
FOR
THE PAY
MULA

In August and September there were strike ballots in two Brigades, West Yorkshire and Greater Manchester.

It worked. A compromise was brokered by Jack Straw. Manchester and West Yorkshire Fire Authorities withdrew proposals to go their own way. The NJC was safe at least until the result of an inquiry, to be conducted by Frank Burchill, Professor of Industrial Relations at Keele University.

Burchill recommended the NJC continue, and proposed a new set of rules about what was for local decision and what was not. The next year, 2000, Burchill became the NJC chairman.

It was Ken Cameron's last battle. That year, he retired.

One of Britain's most active union leaders on the international stage, he counted Nelson Mandela and Fidel Castro among his friends. He was one of the first union leaders to support the Cuba Solidarity Campaign. He proposed the first motion at the TUC – in 1982 – in support of the Palestinians, and helped set up Justice for Colombia.

When he died, 16 years later, the former Unison general secretary Rodney Bickerstaffe wrote in the *Guardian*: "He was humble, principled, funny, generous, wise and fearless."

His successor, 40-year-old Andy Gilchrist, was born and brought up in Bedfordshire and worked at Bedfordshire and Luton FRS from 1979 until 1996, when he became an FBU national officer.

He quickly found that, even though Professor Burchill's conclusions had been accepted by all sides, there were still fire authorities that wanted to evade them.

Merseyside wanted to worsen its firefighters' conditions of service. Agreement was reached after a strike ballot showed 68.5% in favour. Berkshire wanted to impose a new contract. A strike ballot showed 81.6% in favour and the proposal was withdrawn.

Merseyside came back the next year, 2001, with a new way of undermining the national agreement. Its chief fire officer, Malcolm Saunders, decided to put non-uniformed staff into officer posts.

He had what he must have thought was a clever wheeze to wrong-foot the union. The first two non-uniformed staff he put in officers' posts were both members of ethnic minorities. He probably thought that if the union opposed this, he could somehow pin a label on it saying "racist".

None of it worked. In the end Merseyside's FRS backed down.

9/11 and a poisonous cocktail

On 11 September 2001, terrorists flew two aeroplanes, packed with passengers, into two of the tallest buildings in the world, the twin towers of the World Trade Center in New York. The attacks that day killed 2,996 people, and 343 of them were firefighters.

Apart from showing the world the dreadful risks firefighters ran to keep others safe, it seemed also to be the prelude to war. Neither the FBU nor anyone else knew the horrors that would follow, but Gilchrist's comment in the next issue of *Firefighter* showed some foresight:

"Of course there is condemnation of the suicide bombers, of the cruelties and failure of the Iraqi government to address the very real problems of poverty and oppression in their country. But the solution to these problems is not state sponsored violence… You cannot bomb a country into democracy… "

What neither Gilchrist nor anyone else could anticipate was how war in Iraq, and British firefighters' pay and conditions, and the FBU's relationship with Labour, were all about to be mixed into a poisonous cocktail.

Facing page Ken Cameron outside TUC headquarters in London after a conference on strike action, 1993

PRIDE

Right up to the end of the last century, if a firefighter went on a Gay Pride march, their employer would ask them not to wear their uniform, or even their employer's T-shirt.

It's an attitude the union helped to change. After the FBU's Ken Cameron and Ronnie Scott took up the campaign, and an LGBT section was formed within the union, a banner reading "Gay and lesbian firefighters" started to appear on the marches.

"There are still problems out there, but it's a completely different discussion" says Pat Carberry (above left), national secretary of the FBU's LGBT committee. "I used to be the gay firefighter. Now I'm a firefighter who happens to be gay."

CHAPTER SEVEN
WE'RE WORTH IT: THE PAY CAMPAIGN 2002-03

The pay formula – the big gain from the 1977 strike, which tied pay to that of the better-paid male manual workers – served firefighters well for more than two decades.

But in those two decades, skilled manual workers lost out heavily as the traditional industries – mining, steel manufacture, motor manufacturing and the like – suffered huge job losses. So by the turn of the century, the formula was delivering often disappointingly low pay increases. At the same time, firefighting was getting ever more technical, more professional, requiring highly skilled people.

The new general secretary, Andy Gilchrist, argued that the formula was no longer delivering, and firefighters wanted something more.

Many in the FBU felt that the arrival of a Labour government in 1997 after 18 years of Conservative rule would mean they had a more sympathetic ear in Westminster – though Alan McLean suspected right from the start that the new ministers would behave just like the old. "The anti-trade union laws the Tories had brought in were very, very easy to repeal, especially with Labour's huge majority – and they hadn't done it," he says.

A new, more militant mood was fuelled by the London Fire Brigade's decision to discipline 11 firefighters from Homerton fire station in east London. They were suspended on New Year's Day 2000 for defending a longstanding policy of the FBU against prearranged overtime.

Battle lines are drawn…
Big protests and the threat of industrial action accompanied the disciplinary cases, where the firefighters were represented by two London officials who were later to play a major part in the national union, Matt Wrack and Andy Dark. Despite initial threats of dismissal, and in the face of growing militancy among London firefighters, none of the 11 was dismissed.

As the union's pay campaign developed officials looked at wages elsewhere, and developed a case for £30,000 a year

for a firefighter – which meant a 40% increase in 2002. The claim was agreed by the FBU conference that year.

The fire service employers recommended 4%. In response to growing tension in the fire service, the New Labour government commissioned a review into the fire service, chaired by professor George Bain. This suggested 11%, but said it should be conditional on changes to working conditions described as "modernisation".

"When Blair talks about modernisation, he means cuts," said the FBU strike bulletin – an indication of how far relations between the union and the Labour government had broken down.

Ministers and newspapers seized on the 40%, even though Gilchrist was signalling clearly that he was willing to negotiate.

Negotiations stalled, and the union balloted its members on whether they were willing to go on strike. It produced a remarkable result – the biggest endorsement of strike action in any trade union since the union balloting laws were first enacted. 83.5% of the members voted, and of these, 87.6% were in favour and 12.4% against. In Northern Ireland the majority was an extraordinary 96.6%.

The FBU executive council planned for a 48-hour strike in October, and an escalating series of strikes in November and December, including planned eight-day stoppages. Tony Blair's press officer Alastair Campbell wrote in his diary: "I got Godric [Smith, the prime minister's official spokesperson] to do a very tough line on the FBU, no going back to the bad old days."

The first strikes were cancelled to enable negotiations to take place. When talks failed to make a breakthrough, the first strikes were called. Further talks led to the suspension of further strikes.

At one point, at the end of an all-night negotiating session, with an eight-day strike due to start at 9am the next day, the employers offered 16%. John Prescott, who was deputy prime minister as well as environment secretary, was thought to have authorised the offer.

But it was vetoed by chancellor Gordon Brown, who was said by government insiders to be "stamping around Whitehall" demanding that the firefighters be faced down.

Above, top Former mayor of London Ken Livingstone supporting 11 London firefighters suspended in January 2000, for defending the union's long standing policy against pre-arranged overtime. Union rep Linda Smith holds the placard

Above Bridlington, 2002. FBU delegates to the union's annual conference vote to strike for better pay

Facing page A local lad supports striking Leeds firefighters while on their picket line during the national pay strike, 2002-03

Previous page Glasgow, January 2003. Striking firefighters wave to passing motorists tooting their horns in support outside Maryhill fire station during a 48-hour strike

Right FBU pay rally in Belfast, September 2002. Recently retired FBU president Mick Harper marches with his successor Ruth Winters

"We thought we'd got it in the bag," says national officer Dave Green. "We were ready to call it off, and at the 11th hour we were told everything was off, the strike's on. I went back to Nottingham that morning having had no sleep and it was one of the worst days of my trade union life."

In his diary, Alastair Campbell confirmed what happened.

"The unions and the employers did a deal in the early hours. We said no... The FBU and the employers both came out to say we had scuppered the deal... We agreed at the morning meeting to get more on the offensive and we put together some aggressive lines for Godric at the [media briefing], that it beggared belief the employers had signed up to this, that the unions were determined to avoid modernisation. We had to get back on the front foot because the FBU were making all the running."

After that, there was no chance that the negotiators could settle with the union. The government had boxed itself into a corner, and was now determined to take on the union.

It was rigidly committed to its pay policy. It jumped convulsively every time a newspaper reminded it of the winter of discontent. And in the summer, Tony Blair had given a secret undertaking to US president George Bush that Britain would support the US in war against Saddam Hussein's Iraq. "You know, George, whatever you decide to do, I'm with you," he wrote.

"Us and them": Labour bares its teeth

Gilchrist didn't know that. But he was sure the government was planning something it hadn't seen fit to reveal yet. Gordon Brown, said the FBU strike bulletin: "has no money for essential public services like the fire service but plenty for warmongering. Yesterday... the chancellor said he'd set aside £1 billion for a war on Iraq, or 'international defence responsibilities' as he puts it."

If he was going to lead the country into an unpopular war, the last thing Blair needed was a firefighters' strike. The FBU either had to be given enough to prevent it or, if Brown would not allow that, they had to be beaten.

Brown wouldn't allow a settlement. So Blair took personal charge, as Campbell's diary confirms: "JP

[Prescott] came to see me to discuss fire and whether he should meet [Andy] Gilchrist." It's significant that the deputy prime minister had to ask the prime minister's press secretary whether he could meet Gilchrist.

"Prescott was doing a statement which I rewrote during Cabinet, giving him some cover by making clear that if we moved from a two-day to an eight-day strike, we were in a different ball game and some issues that had been kept off the table to suit them when we were trying to avert the strike would then be on the table.

"JP was up for doing the tough stuff if we had to. He was very on board at the moment, just took the changes, including a sound-bite that said we had bent over backwards and been met with a response that was wrong, irresponsible and puts lives at risk."

Campbell claimed to be: "outraged at the way they were using fire service buildings to plan the strikes, to protest, but then go inside when it rained".

In parliament, Blair said the aborted settlement would have cost £500 million. The true figure was about £70 million, but the nation was not yet used to Blair's creative ways with facts. He invented a figure of £16 billion as the cost to the economy if the firefighters' increase was applied across the public sector.

Campbell rallied the media against the firefighters. It didn't need much encouragement. "We never really

"SADDAM'S FRIENDS"

In 2002 Ruth Winters became the union's first woman president, and played a central part in the strike.

She was also one of the key speakers at the demonstration against the looming Iraq War, alongside Reverend Jesse Jackson, Tony Benn, Liberal Democrat leader Charles Kennedy, writer Tariq Ali, ex-minister Mo Mowlam, London's mayor Ken Livingstone, actor Vanessa Redgrave and playwright Harold Pinter.

The union's stand led Bernard Jenkin, then Conservative MP for North Essex, to label FBU members "Saddam's friends".

quite understood the hostility with which the established press would attack us," says another national official, John McGhee.

An uneasy truce: an end to strike action

We now know that News International, which owned the *Sun*, the *Times* and the now-defunct *News of the World*, was illegally tapping the telephones of Andy Gilchrist, John McGhee and Ken Cameron. This enabled them to follow the union's leadership everywhere, to turn up in any pub they might be drinking in, any restaurant they might be eating in. People started knocking on the door of Gilchrist's home, where his wife and two young children lived. The union had to arrange security systems for the house.

At one meeting, after Gilchrist had been spied on and made to look salacious by News International papers, he turned up for a meeting with John Prescott the next morning. "I'm sorry, Andy," said Prescott. Gilchrist brushed it aside, but Prescott persisted: "No, I'm really sorry." What did he mean? "How do I know?" says Gilchrist now. "So it was MI5, or Campbell, or all or none of them? You can't worry about it."

But we do know that Campbell, in his own words, was: "taking a hands-on interest in story development on fire".

The union's leadership was even more worried by social media, then in its infancy.

It had helped fund the creation of a campaign website, but was horrified to find that opponents among firefighters used it to criticise the way the dispute was being handled. Some complained about the way strikes were on and then off, about the fear that an eventual settlement would fall way below the claim, and much else.

At the same time, the union ran a modern and sophisticated communications operation for the strike. Surprised industrial correspondents found themselves welcome on picket lines, standing around the striking firefighters' braziers, and learning more about their case than any number of official press statements could have told them.

As the relentless media onslaught started to rattle the FBU leadership, Campbell's diaries reveal growing

Above A cartoon of former Labour prime minister Tony Blair in the June 2002 issue of *Firefighter* magazine

satisfaction, and John Prescott was told to prepare legislation giving him power to downsize the fire service and dictate pay and conditions.

In April, Frank Burchill produced a set of proposals designed to form the basis of a settlement.

The next month, there was a new offer. It would give a 16% pay rise, but over three years, and a two-year pay formula linking firefighters with professional and technical workers rather than manual workers. It was rather like the offer Gordon Brown had vetoed early on – but this time firmly linked to "modernisation".

FBU members had cracked that code long ago. "Modernisation" meant ripping up the conditions of service, national standards, crewing levels and duty systems that the union had fought for since 1918 and particularly since the creation of the modern service after the Second World War.

As if it wasn't clear enough, John Prescott told the House of Commons of the government's intention to repeal section 19 of the Fire Services Act 1947. That was the section which prevented local fire services from cutting jobs or closing fire stations without the secretary of state's consent. Prescott said it made "modernisation" more difficult.

But the alternative to "modernisation", ministers told FBU negotiators, was that the government would take control and impose a settlement.

Andy Gilchrist wrote in the strike bulletin: "This offer is a good opportunity to put the pay campaign behind us so we can prepare ourselves for the future battles to defend our fire service."

Senior managers were already cutting the number of appliances and calling it modernisation.

The union was fiercely divided about the offer, but, at a conference in Glasgow called especially to discuss it, it was accepted.

It was a controversial end to a strike that had divided the union. Opponents said the strings attached to the pay rise meant giving away the fire service that had been fought for and won under John Horner's leadership after the war and in subsequent decades. The government would now be free to erode national standards and conditions of work.

Its defenders said that a 16% pay rise – even if phased – was a lot more than had been on offer before the strike, and provided a better platform for the future.

They added that the strings attached to the deal would have come anyway – they were part of New Labour's agenda.

And on New Labour, the FBU was united. New Labour had betrayed firefighters. The political party of the trade union movement had lined up with their enemies.

End of an era: severing links and regrouping

The executive wanted to give New Labour another chance. But the 2004 conference disagreed.

Tony Maguire of Northern Ireland spoke for many when he told the conference: "Our party, the party we nurtured through the Thatcher years, the party that we kept the faith with in the eighties and nineties, and the party that trade unionists like us gave millions of pounds to – and for what? To be stabbed, not in the back, but in the heart."

After 78 years, the FBU disaffiliated from the Labour Party.

That year, the Fire and Rescue Services Act tore up the postwar settlement. The Central Fire Brigades Advisory Council was abolished and nothing equivalent was put in its place. Ever since then the FBU has had to fight "modernisation" locally, cut by cut.

The next year, Gilchrist came up for re-election. The big election issue was the handling of the strike, and he lost decisively to Matt Wrack.

A sitting general secretary had never been thrown out before. A new leadership team emerged, as Wrack was joined by assistant general secretary Andy Dark and president Mick Shaw.

FBU: "THE DRIVING FORCE FOR EQUALITY"

Born in East London to African-Caribbean parents, Micky Nicholas (seen below – back row left) joined the London Fire Brigade in 1990, aged 26. One of his worst moments as a new firefighter was when Dave Stokoe, a firefighter he had trained with, was one of two firefighters who died at the Gillender Street fire.

Nicholas quickly became an FBU representative, and then secretary of the black and ethnic minority members (B&EMM) section. Just before the 2002 strike, he took up the newly created B&EMM seat on the executive.

The B&EMM section had evolved from a national meeting at Wortley Hall, Sheffield. "It was what we call in the fire service a great big gripe meeting," Nicholas says. He maintains that within two years the FBU had become the driving force for equality in the fire service.

There was racism in the fire service, but it was unthinking, he says. "Some people didn't know black people, they didn't live in the same communities, and it was almost a fear of the unknown."

Above The national B&EMM committee at the FBU annual conference, Bridlington, May 2003

Facing page June 2002's national pay rally ends with thousands of firefighters assembling in Trafalgar Square to listen to speeches by, among others, George Galloway MP and Brendan Barber of the TUC

Above Glasgow, May 2004. The Stockline Plastics factory explosion caused nine fatalities and was the worst industrial disaster in Scotland since the Piper Alpha oil rig explosion and fire in 1988. The operators ICL Plastics and ICL Tech were fined £400,000 and pleaded guilty to breaching health and safety legislation and admitted four offences that led to the explosion at their factory

Right Hertfordshire, December 2005. The explosion at the Buncefield fuel depot (Hertfordshire Oil Storage Limited (HOSL)) was the largest since the Second World War and was heard as far away as France, Belgium and the Netherlands. It took 180 firefighters, 53m litres of water, 180,000 litres of foam and 30km of high volume hose, five days to extinguish the fire. Of the 43 casualties, two were seriously injured and miraculously there were no fatalities. The explosion occurred due to a faulty gauge which allowed one of the tanks to overfill. The secondary containment system also failed and 250,000 litres of petrol overflowed from the top of the tank causing a vapour cloud which ignited.

HOSL, a company controlled by oil conglomerates, Total and Chevron, was found guilty of grave safety failures. The guilty verdict followed one of the most complex corporate criminal trials of its kind and was a major blow for Total, the major shareholder

CHAPTER EIGHT
A FIRE AND RESCUE SERVICE UNDER ATTACK

Matt Wrack grew up in Manchester but joined the fire service in London in 1983.

After attending Southwark Training Centre he worked at Silvertown and then Kingsland fire stations in east London – all three, as he now points out ruefully, closed by Boris Johnson when he was mayor of London.

Wrack was an FBU activist from the start, and during the 2002 strike he was London regional organiser and a severe critic of the leadership strategy. A year after he became general secretary, he was elected to the general council of the TUC.

As the new general secretary in 2005 he faced a radically changed fire service. The Central Fire Brigades Advisory Council (CFBAC), which had been established in 1947, and through which the union worked to professionalise the fire service, was scrapped. The pay formula, which had come out of the 1977 national strike, was gone.

The pay formula had meant that there did not have to be an annual dogfight over pay. This allowed the union to put its energies into making firefighting safer and more professional.

Now everything had changed. Andy Dark, elected assistant general secretary the same year, says: "We now had a situation where each FRS set its own standards and training. One FRS will send one pump to a certain sort of incident, another will send four. It's a postcode lottery. Response times can be whatever they want and we have seen them creeping up. There's a wide range of duty systems."

The settlement reached in 2003 was a five-year deal lasting until 2007.

New ways of influencing government policy had to be found. A new FBU parliamentary group was formed, with John McDonnell MP as secretary. Jeremy Corbyn was a founder member.

Wrack and Dark had hardly got their feet under the table when terrorists bombed the London underground and a London bus, killing 52 people and injuring 700.

In the middle of the rush hour, three bombs were detonated on board London underground trains within 50 seconds of each other. An hour later, a bomb detonated on a bus. Wrack reflected in *Firefighter*:

"Those who were helping did not inquire as to the race or religion of those to whom they were offering the hand of humanity . . . I am sure all FBU members were proud of the role that firefighters play…

"In a sense we should not expect any acknowledgement – the fire service did what it is trained to do. But as always happens, firefighters will have given far more than what is required by training… Yet my pride at the professionalism and compassion of our members… is also tinged with some anger. I am angry that our service remains under attack. In London itself the fire authority has agreed cuts in central London stations… "

Tragedy strikes as cuts take effect

It was not just London. Local fire services were embarking with enthusiasm on "modernisation" proposals that the 2004 act now permitted. So there were more local disputes than at any time in the union's history.

Sometimes it was the imposition of shift patterns that made family life for a firefighter almost impossible, as in the West Midlands. Sometimes it was firefighter numbers – in Hertfordshire, firefighters went on strike over threats to 40 jobs. Strike action in Merseyside in 2006 was against a plan to slash £3.5 million from the budget by axing 120 frontline firefighter posts.

The Hertfordshire strike came just 18 months after two Hertfordshire firefighters died in a 16-storey block of flats in Stevenage.

In a 14th-floor flat, a young couple had run out of cash credits for the electricity. So they placed a candle on the television, and it caught fire in the small hours. Around 70 people were evacuated as intense heat melted window frames and flames spread to the floors above.

Firefighters Michael Millar, 26, from Stevenage, and Jeff Wornham, 28, from Royston, saved the young man from the fire on the 14th floor, and went back for the young woman. They died trying, unsuccessfully, to save her too.

Howard Millar, Michael Millar's father, said: "I don't believe that the tragedy had anything to do with individual

Above 7/7 London bombings, 2005. Firefighters and other emergency personnel carry an injured person from Aldgate tube station

Facing page In August 2011, firefighters battled one blaze every nine minutes for five consecutive days during the London riots. Triggered by the fatal shooting of Mark Duggan, rioting then spread to other locations across England

Previous page Firefighters at work in Baildon Bridge, Shipley, West Yorkshire, 2015. It was flooded by the River Aire which broke its banks when the water reached record levels after heavy rains over the Christmas period

errors but was directly because Hertfordshire Fire and Rescue Service – like so many others across the UK – have not been giving their fire crews the hands-on training and preparation needed."

An FBU investigation concluded that Hertfordshire FRS did not have proper procedures or provide adequate training, and did not send enough firefighters in the initial response. The coroner called for Hertfordshire FRS to work with the FBU to ensure lessons were learned.

It was part of a sudden spike in firefighter deaths. The next year, 2006, 63-year-old Brian Wembridge, a retired firefighter working for the fire service as a video technician, and firefighter Geoff Wicker, 49, died at Marlie Farm, Ringmer, East Sussex.

The owner of the farm, Martin Winter, omitted to tell firefighters he was storing fireworks in a shipping container. He said the container had only wood in it. So fire crews were trying to set up a pump to cool the container when they should have evacuated.

Moments before the box exploded and killed him, Brian Wembridge shot film which later helped convict Winter and his son of manslaughter through gross negligence.

A new low: 2007/08 and calls for reform

The FBU launched a case for compensation on behalf of the family of Brian Wembridge. East Sussex Fire and Rescue Service mounted the startling argument that, because firefighting is a dangerous profession, safety regulations should not apply and the FRS could not be said to have a duty of care.

The FBU won – a key victory, because if East Sussex FRS had got away with that argument, fire and rescue services would have been able to avoid any responsibility for safety on the fire ground.

East Sussex FRS appealed against the decision, and managed to delay paying the compensation for ten years.

In 2007 came the biggest loss of firefighters' lives for 35 years, since seven died in Kilbirnie Street, Glasgow, in 1972.

Watch manager Ian Reid, 44, and firefighter John Averis, 27, from Stratford upon Avon fire station, died alongside firefighters Ashley Stephens, 21, and Darren Yates-Badley, 24, from Alcester station, in a fire at an industrial estate in Atherstone on Stour, Warwickshire.

About 100 firefighters and five ambulance crews went to the blaze at the site owned by Wealmoor Atherstone Ltd. The company employed 300 workers. A sprinkler system had been fitted but not been made operational.

When firefighters first arrived, no smoke or flames were visible from the outside. But there was a lot of flammable material inside.

Because of the layout of the building, firefighters were unable to reach the fire in the early stages to extinguish it. The fire became very severe very fast, and the four firefighters were killed by intense heat.

Warwickshire County Council was fined £30,000 after a week-long hearing at Stafford Crown Court. The fire service had failed to distribute information about buildings and water supplies, said the court, and training of firefighters was inadequate.

The Warwickshire deaths, according to an FBU report in 2008, "together with other deaths in Strathclyde, North Wales, Hertfordshire, Dumfries and Galloway and Central Scotland, make 2007-8 an unprecedented year for firefighter deaths in recent times. Nine firefighters died on duty between April 2007 and March 2008."

The research showed that, while deaths at fires had virtually ceased in the late 1990s, they were now rising sharply. And they were "consistently linked to failures in the risk assessment process".

The main reason, the report found, was inadequate risk assessment. Poor training was also a factor. And there was too little guidance being issued on operational matters and reflecting changes to the risk firefighters faced.

Previously, guidance issued by the Central Fire Brigades Advisory Council had considerable influence on how local fire services planned for risk. Now the service was being increasingly fragmented, with different approaches adopted in different services.

The FBU report called for a national independent fire and rescue service investigation unit, and for: "centrally issued, substantial, safety critical national guidance".

EWAN WILLIAMSON

The funeral of 35-year-old firefighter Ewan Williamson, green watch, Tollcross fire station, who died while attending a fire in an Edinburgh pub on 12 July 2009. He was the only firefighter in the history of Lothian and Borders Fire and Rescue Service to die in the line of duty.

The FBU released a fatal accident investigation report that made 14 recommendations to the Scottish FRS. It included policy on the use of breathing apparatus and tactical ventilation of buildings. Most of the recommendations have been adopted.

Facing page The aftermath of an explosion at Marlie Farm, East Sussex, 3 December 2006. The owner of the farm omitted to tell firefighters he was storing fireworks

Other reports followed: into attacks on firefighters, floods, emergency response times. The union argued that the shift towards "localism" and the ending of national standards and inspection were creating an increasingly fragmented fire and rescue service.

But local fire services seemed more interested in what the government called modernisation, and what the FBU called cuts. In 2009, in what was a first in the fire service, South Yorkshire FRS began the process of the dismissal and re-engagement of 744 firefighters in order to impose new shift arrangements.

The employers wanted 12-hour day and night shifts to replace the existing 15-hour night shifts and nine-hour day shifts. The discontinuous strikes ended when the National Joint Council joint secretaries were brought in and brokered a settlement.

The next year, the London Fire Brigade tried the same tactic, starting formal proceedings to dismiss and re-engage 5,500 firefighters.

During the Hertfordshire strike, the government had stopped the practice of utilising the army for providing fire cover. So in London, for the first time, the employers brought in a private company as a strikebreaking force. London Fire Brigade had signed a £9m deal with AssetCo.

The immediate result was that AssetCo drivers instigated violence on the picket line. Vehicles driven by strikebreakers knocked down three FBU members.

Croydon firefighter Tamer Ozdemir was airlifted to hospital with pelvic injuries after he was hit by a speeding car driven by a station manager at Croydon fire station. FBU president Mick Shaw, who was there, described what happened:

"As the pickets tried to talk to the driver of the car, it accelerated suddenly and one of the striking firefighters was thrown up and into the windscreen, then several feet in front of the car."

A fire engine was deliberately driven at the FBU London executive council member Ian Leahair, one of a group of peaceful pickets at Southwark fire station. Leahair was shaken and bruised but not seriously injured.

And Dagenham firefighter Graham Beers held his hand up at the side of a road in Southwark, to signal to the crew of a fire engine being returned to Southwark fire station that they should stop and speak to him. "The fire engine swerved towards me and hit my hand," said Beers.

The strike ended with the withdrawal of the dismissal notices and a compromise on new shift patterns.

The union then fought a series of station closures in London.

For Matt Wrack, this was personal. Southwark Training Centre, where he had trained – "a wonderful place, now being sold off," he said bitterly – was closed, and he found himself demonstrating outside Kingsland fire station, where he had worked – also being closed.

"I joined the fire service in 1983," he wrote in *Firefighter* in October 2007. "On my recruitment course we learned about the structure of the fire service. And that meant the 1947 Fire Services Act, a local service working to national standards… And it meant a pension scheme created about the same time. In the past five years we have seen the whole pack of cards thrown into the air…

"Looming over the entire service is the massively expensive and flawed plan to regionalise emergency fire control."

Whitehall farce and FBU fightback

This was a plan to reduce England's 46 fire control centres to nine. FBU control staff had warned all along that it would never work, and millions of pounds were being wasted on the rent and upkeep of buildings earmarked for it, but unused. The project was dogged with technical problems and delays.

As Sharon Riley, former FBU executive council member for control staff, said: "Over the last seven years the FBU has been the only consistent voice of opposition to the project."

The FBU was vindicated. In December 2010 the new coalition government realised it was a disaster and cancelled it.

That was a plus. But there was a serious minus too. Many fire services were left with aging mobilising systems. They

PRIVATISATION FIASCO

In addition to its contract for strikebreaking, AssetCo also had a contract with Abu Dhabi, whose fire services it ran. And fire authorities handed the company a 20-year PFI contract to own and maintain all fire appliances in London and Lincolnshire.

Matt Wrack warned London fire commissioner Ron Dobson of the danger. But Dobson went ahead with the deal. And all London's fire appliances were under threat when the company got into financial difficulties.

The company's accountants were fined £2.4 million and the Financial Reporting Council said that its three top directors acted: "dishonestly or recklessly".

The fire engines were for a time owned by one of AssetCo's creditors, Lloyds TSB. They were eventually sold to an eccentric peer for £2.

Facing page Lobby of Westminster by firefighter control members against attacks by government on jobs and conditions, October 2009

Above Family support for a national firefighters rally against attacks on their pensions, 2014

Facing page Smethwick plastic recycling plant, 2013. More than 200 firefighters attended the huge fire involving 100,000 tonnes of plastic recycling material

had not updated them because they were expecting a new regional control centre to take over.

With the project now cancelled, they sought alternatives to replace their existing systems. The answer for some was ad hoc mergers with neighbouring fire services, and in the North West, four fire services formed the first arms-length company]control centre.

The new government also wanted to reduce fire-service pensions, along with all public-sector pensions.

The previous government had tried to nibble away at them. In May 2009 the Court of Appeal stopped some proposed new regulations that would have allowed brigades to sack disabled and badly injured firefighters without a pension or redundancy.

The court found in favour of three London firefighters, backed by the FBU, whose ill health and injury pensions had been removed when the government changed the guidance.

But that was a skirmish. The war was on its way. The new government wanted to raise the age at which firefighters could retire from 55 to 60.

The union pointed out the physical demands of the job. "We decided to run an evidence-based campaign," said Matt Wrack. "We cannot expect large numbers of firefighters in their late 50s to fight fires and rescue families without creating danger to the public and firefighters."

Injustice, action and unrest: 2013 onwards

The government also wanted fewer firefighters. All told, 1500 firefighter jobs went in 2010 – the first year of the new government – a year in which two more firefighters died.

Shirley Towers in Southampton had already been identified as a risk, partly because of its unusual design. James Shears, 35, and Alan Bannon, 38, went into flat 72 on the ninth floor to support two other firefighters already inside and searching for the seat of the fire.

The fire intensified. Their two colleagues made it out, badly burned. Shears and Bannon, trapped by fallen cables, did not.

Five years later the council at last put sprinklers into three of the city's tower blocks, and new regulations required

that wiring systems must use metal and not plastic to keep cables in place in escape routes.

It should have been done earlier. Fallen cables had been identified as a factor in the deaths of firefighters Michael Millar and Jeff Wornham in Hertfordshire, five years before the Southampton fire.

In 2013, three years after the Southampton fire, firefighter and former soldier Stephen Hunt, 38, died in a fire in Manchester. He was one of 60 firefighters responding to a fire at Paul's Hair World in Oldham Street.

He and his BA partner were enveloped by a sudden surge of extreme heat. This may have been fuelled by the chemicals stored at the business, which supplied hair extensions and hair beauty products.

Both were taken to hospital. Stephen Hunt was declared dead on arrival.

A huge fire at a Smethwick plastic recycling plant the same year exposed the dangers of fire service cuts. The blaze: "stretched the service to breaking point," wrote the West Midlands executive member Rose Jones in *Firefighter*.

"Those involved in fighting the fire made it clear that government cuts have hampered their ability to deal with major incidents. Some firefighters were required to spend excessive time (in some cases 12 hours) in extremely difficult and dangerous conditions.

"Fire engines were sent from Stafford and Malvern to compensate for shortages… The West Midlands FRS has recently experienced a 26% (or £20 million) cut to its budget and a 22% reduction in the number of firefighters (from 1,850 to 1,450)… Several of the fire engines which fought the blaze will be lost to the cuts in a matter of weeks."

What was true of the West Midlands was also true for the rest of the country.

It had become clear that reasoned argument on pensions wasn't working. The government was "rushing on with legislation to make firefighters pay more, work longer and still get less," as Matt Wrack put it in *Firefighter*. The union balloted members on strike action, and 78% voted yes.

The dispute was the longest in the history of the FBU – a series of strikes, demonstrations, lobbies and mass rallies, a parliamentary debate and a legal challenge.

Above Matt Wrack speaking at the Durham Miners' Gala in 2017 alongside Labour leader Jeremy Corbyn

Facing page London, 2007. A spectacular rescue of a man as he attempts to commit suicide by jumping from Millennium bridge

As we write, the legal challenge to the government proposals is still working its way through the courts. The last strike was in 2015, when a Recall conference decided against further strikes.

In 2015, Sian Griffiths retired as watch manager in Paddington. She wrote in *Firefighter* that the dangers of her job were brought home to her two years after she became a firefighter. She arrived at the 1987 King's Cross fire to see colleagues carrying someone out.

"I realised that that person was a firefighter because they had a tunic on. Then I recognised it was Colin [Station Officer Colin Townsley, who died there]. But she criticised those politicians, responsible for imposing cuts and scrapping standards, "namely those people that have never worked for the fire service, (who) seem to treat us with contempt. That is why it is so important to have a union."

And some things had got better. "When I joined the London Fire Brigade as a firefighter [in 1985] there were five women," she said. "There are now 333."

There are also more black firefighters. That was all work for which the FBU provided the platform and the opportunity.

A new hope? Looking to the future

There was another reason to be optimistic in 2015, according to Matt Wrack. Labour's defeat in the general election was followed by the even more surprising election of Jeremy Corbyn as Labour leader. It marked a clear break from the Blair years in which Labour had turned its fire on its own people and on the FBU.

The FBU reaffiliated to the Labour Party after an absence of 11 years. "When the Corbyn phenomenon happened, I thought at once: we need to be in the thick of this," Wrack says.

Corbyn told Firefighter: "Firefighters protect us, look after us. Their treatment from the government has been appalling."

So what now, at the start of the union's second century?

The Fire Brigades Union has faced a long term attack; on all fronts. Governments, local politicians and many chief fire officers have attempted to undermine standards

as a mechanism to allow cuts to be forced through. The improvements in professionalism and in standards made after the Second World War have been undermined.

But today the Fire Brigades Union continues to campaign for something better. Investment in the fire service, so that there are enough stations, enough equipment and enough firefighters. National standards.

A pay formula so that firefighters are not forced into the world of low pay and state benefits that afflicted the service in the 1970s. That way, the union's energies can go into campaigning for better safety, better training, greater professionalism.

A fit-for-purpose pension scheme based on the firefighter's occupation.

A broader role for firefighters – but introduced on a professional basis, with pay and training to match. The firefighter of the future will be increasingly involved with fire prevention as well as firefighting and with tackling a whole range of other risks. Firefighters will make even greater contributions to public safety than they make now.

It's a besieged, defiant but optimistic and determined union that enters its second century.

---

100 YEARS OLD, AND STILL BREAKING RECORDS

FBU research shows that firefighters rescued more people than ever before during the period April 2016 to March 2017.

A record 43,000 people were rescued throughout the UK for the period, a 6% increase on the previous year. The rise is largely due to an increase in non-fire rescues, from incidents such as flooding, hazardous chemical spillages and road traffic collisions. More than 39,000 rescues were carried out from non-fire incidents, and 4,000 people were rescued from fires.

POSTSCRIPT

GRENFELL

At 12:54 on 14 June 2017, the first 999 call came into the London Fire Brigade. There was a fire at a 24-storey tower block called Grenfell Tower in West London.

The first fire crews were there in six minutes. The fire was in a fourth floor flat.

Watch manager Mike Dowden, from North Kensington fire station, took charge. He ordered crews into the building to fight the fire and those outside to secure the water supply.

Crew manager Charlie Batterbee and firefighter Dan Brown entered the flat in breathing apparatus (BA), searched for casualties and found a fierce fire. They managed to extinguish the fire inside the flat within fifteen minutes.

Watch manager Brien O'Keeffe, in charge at the bridgehead, said:

"It was a very quick attack actually. I thought 'good job'…And then, in what seemed like seconds… it all changed… The crew transmitted that there was smoke on the fifth floor. They went to the fifth and then they went to the sixth. From that moment onwards, we just started carrying out rescues. I committed as much BA as I could at that time."

Inside the original flat, Brown climbed on to a counter to try to extinguish the blaze, which had spread outside the building. Batterbee said: "I held on to him by his breathing apparatus set shoulder strap as he lent out the window on the fourth floor with the jet. Brown started hitting it with the jet, but it was having no effect."

From the ground, other firefighters tried to stop the fire spread, but without success. By 01.26, the fire had reached the 23rd floor of the building. It had taken just 12 minutes.

Breathing apparatus crews were sent in to the building to fight the fire and to carry out rescues.

Crew managers Guy Tillotson and Ben Gallagher and firefighters Harry Bettinson and Jim Wolfenden reached the ninth floor. They woke up a woman and her seven-year-old daughter. Thick, black smoke outside their flat blocked their escape. Two firefighters stayed in the flat while the others went to fetch more breathing apparatus sets to use for the residents.

Bettinson, still on probation, said: "We put one of the new sets on the mum so she was wearing it on her back. Then I got a spare mask set out and I hooked this up…so the little girl would be breathing my air.

They descended through the thick smoke down the tight stairwell. Outside, they ran the gauntlet of falling debris to move casualties away from the inferno, using police riots shields for protection.

An hour into the fire, control room operator Peter Duddy took a call from a man on the 12th floor, who said the smoke was thick and his family could not get out. He had two children, aged eight and 12, with him and he could hear the fire in the flat next door. He said that there was fire outside his flat and pleaded with Duddy to come and get him and his daughters.

At the bridgehead, watch manager Louisa De SiIvo briefed firefighters David Hill and Abdul Malik to get to the 12th floor to rescue the family. On their way up the firefighters

became separated. At 02:32 Hill made it to the 12th floor and found the flat. He told the family to get some wet towels and put them over their mouths, as it would be hard to breath. He lined them up and told them to hold onto each other and follow him.

As soon as the family left flat 95 the children began screaming that they could not breathe. Hill removed his helmet and facemask and tried to give the four people air from his own equipment. He picked up one of the daughters and ran down the stairs with her to clean air, where he handed her to another firefighter.

He then ran back up the stairs to locate the rest of the family. He found a casualty. His warning whistle began to sound, indicating he was short of air. He got the casualty to the bridgehead and returned again looking for casualties. On the verge of collapse, Hill was assisted out by firefighter Gemma Bloxham.

As the sun rose in London, smoke was pouring into the morning sky. Reports emerged of people signalling with torches from the top floor of the building, tying bedsheets together to climb down, hammering on windows for help.

Seventy two people lost their lives. Over two hundred firefighters responded through the night. They fought a fire in a building where every element of fire protection failed; the fire doors, the windows, the smoke extraction system, the fire lifts. And, of course, the building was wrapped in highly flammable cladding. They rescued as many people as they could and they rescued many. They are still haunted by those they could not reach.

On 14 June 2017, in a 24-storey tower block, a fire that started in a fourth floor flat went on to claim 72 lives, the worst fire in terms of fire deaths in living memory in the UK

"THAT'S WHAT TRADE UNIONISTS LOOK LIKE"

FBU General Secretary Matt Wrack's speech, Durham Miners' Gala 2017

FRIENDS, sisters, brothers, comrades, it is an honour to be here once again to speak on behalf of the Fire Brigades Union to the "Big Meeting".

I want to add our voice to the tributes to Davey Hopper, a true working-class hero who is very much missed across our movement. He was a great friend to us in the FBU and indeed to all of those engaged in trade-union and working-class struggle.

He was also a unique master of the English language and particularly that part of it which originated in old Anglo-Saxon.

And we know that Davey and Davey Guy before him would want this wonderful, working-class, labour movement festival to continue and go from strength to strength, and I know that with your commitment, it will do so.

Now, I'm here today to speak specifically, about the terrible fire at Grenfell Tower.

And I know the thoughts of all of you will be with all those affected, particularly those who lost family and friends on that awful night.

I know that, like millions around the country, you will be full of praise for those who responded to the calls for help through 999 calls that night.

Those in the London Fire Brigade; the ambulance service; police officers who shielded firefighters entering the building from falling and burning debris; the council workers who tried to pick up the pieces afterwards; our remarkable hospital staff in our National Health Service.

We know also, that in the aftermath of this there was a remarkable community response. A huge effort, organised by people on the ground to look after those affected – even while those in authority at local and national level utterly failed to do so.

I want to say something about our members, the firefighters, that night. I have spoken to quite a few, but by no means all.

I was a firefighter for more than two decades and I've been around this industry now for 34 years and I have never, in my professional life, seen firefighters have to deal with a fire on that scale and with such a risk to life.

I have never seen firefighters have to do the things that they did on that terrible night.

Firefighting is based on planning for risks. But the scale of the fire at Grenfell Tower was not planned for...because it should never have happened.

In those circumstances firefighters simply could not apply the normal practices and procedures that enable them to do their job effectively in other emergency incidents.

One firefighter described to me that the many, many decades of knowledge, skills,

Above A minutes silence for victims of the Grenfell Tower fire

training and experience were brought to bear by the hundreds of people there to try to deal with a situation that nobody had prepared for and that nobody expected.

Our procedures are there to enable firefighters to intervene, to save lives, to tackle fires and other emergencies.

They have developed over many years and are based on knowledge, equipment and experience.

They enable firefighters to enter burning buildings when other people are trying to get out.

But firefighting equipment and personal protection do not turn those people into superheroes – they remain human beings.

We had firefighters who became lost from their colleagues; teams that became split.

We had firefighters whose air ran out while they were trying to save lives.

We had firefighters who gave their own safety equipment to members of the public.

We had firefighters who entered that building again and again – against normal safe working practices – and why was that?

Because they were determined to try to do what they could to save lives and to do whatever was possible. And that night they did...they did consciously and deliberately risk their own lives in order to save others.

It is a miracle, indeed, that we did not lose significant numbers of our own members that night. They did save lives. But tragically many people, far, far too many people died.

And firefighters would say this: that they are proud to do that job. They are proud of their trade...It means that they will go into buildings like that knowing not what they might find but relying on their skills, their knowledge, their training and above all their teamwork in order to do that service for the public.

And I would also say this about firefighters, and other people who responded that night: they're also workers.

And they are also, by the way, members of a trade union. And... almost to a man and a woman the people going into that building were members of the Fire Brigades Union (FBU).

So the next time the press turn on us, take a moment; and look at the pictures of those firefighters queuing up in their breathing apparatus, to enter that inferno. And remind them... that's what trade unionists look like.

Now we... in the FBU... stand... in solidarity...with the victims of this appalling and horrifying event. We demand a full and accountable and open inquiry where the victims, and those who attempted their rescue, are at the heart of that process.

Because...this was no act of God. There was no higher power that ordained this event should or could happen.

We live in a wealthy country. We live in a country with a huge knowledge of building construction. We have world-leading experts on fire safety in this country. So this should not happen here – but it did happen here.

This is a country that can send remote controlled guided missiles turning corners down streets half way across the world but we can't keep people safe in their own homes.

We have the right, therefore, to ask questions and to demand answers – and we have the right to demand action as a result of those questions and that process.

We will find, as we examine this incident, that indeed this was no act of God but rather, this is the result of a series of decisions, a series, yes, of political decisions, that created this situation where this could happen.

When there is a concerted attack over many, many years on council housing; when local authority building control is decimated and privatised; when fire safety inspecting officers in the fire service are reduced by more than half so that fire inspections are also reduced to that degree; when public fire research is virtually eliminated in this country; when the government launches attack after attack on so-called "red tape"; when a prime minister describes health and safety as a "monster" that must be slain; when local authority budgets are cut to pieces; when the fire and rescue service is devastated by cuts; when a former mayor of London, Boris Johnson, can say to someone challenging him over closing 10 fire stations to "get stuffed" and think it's all a big joke; when all national standards in our fire and rescue service have been abolished; when the views of front line workers in housing departments or firefighters are regularly dismissed as "special interests"; when all these things happen over the years, then you create the environment when this terrible, terrible

Above, top
Firefighters resting at the scene of the fire

Above Firefighters at Grenfell Tower being given some overhead cover from falling debris by the police

tragedy can happen and for us, therefore, this needs to be a turning point.

And the best tribute that we can pay to those who lost their lives...is to fight for justice and fight for a major change of direction to ensure that this never happens again, and that means ending the relentless attack on public safety. Ending the attack on public services. That means ending the long-term attack on public housing.

So when they ask: Is this a direct result of austerity? I say: It's somewhat more complex than that.

But it is a result of three decades of political assault on the public sector and public services and on those who deliver them. It is a result of three decades of telling us that the market is supreme and we should run our public services as well as though we were running a supermarket.

And far from being a solution, those ideas and that system helped create this mess. They are wrecking our public services just like, in 2007/8, they wrecked the world economy.

And instead of their approach, we look to the founding principles of this movement that we can see reflected on the beautiful and magnificent banners that lead us in to the "Big Meeting" today.

The people who built our movement, the people who built the trade unions, carried in their hearts and in their heads the idea of a better way of doing things, that puts people before profit; that is based on human solidarity, not the narrow interests of a tiny minority; it was called socialism.

We need to discuss that today and organise for it tomorrow.

Solidarity forever!

INDEX

Overleaf, right A wreath laying ceremony in honour of fallen firefighters was the first in a series of commemorative events celebrated during the union's centenary on 13 October 2018

Overleaf, left After the wreath laying ceremony at the National Firefighters Memorial, the FBU pipe band led the procession of union members from across the UK across the Millennium Bridge to Southwark Cathedral

AUTHOR'S ACKNOWLEDGEMENTS

I want to thank the FBU, its executive council and its general secretary Matt Wrack, for entrusting their story to me to tell, and helping me tell it.

I'm grateful to Helen Hague, distinguished former industrial correspondent, who did a lot of preliminary work for this book and handed over to me all the fruits of her labours and film makers Alison Rooper and Winstan Witter, who shared their diligent research into FBU history.

Key FBU people, present and past, have given me revealing and interesting interviews: Andy Dark, Mike Fordham, Andy Gilchrist, Dave Green, John McGhee, Alan McLean, Micky Nicholas and Matt Wrack.

Over the years I've had the pleasure and privilege to be closely associated with the union, and with its staff and activists.

I've learned from all of them. There are too many to list. But two of the communications team have been closely involved at every stage: then head of communications Lynne Wallis, and Anna Zych, who is this book's picture editor, as well as being, for many years, the key to the union's communications operation.

FBU archivist Amy Gardener and all the staff in the Modern Records Centre at Warwick University have been kind and helpful.

BIBLIOGRAPHY

Bailey, Victor (ed), Forged in Fire (Lawrence and Wishart, 1992)
Beckett, Francis, Firefighters and the Blitz (Merlin, 2010.)
Demarne, Cyril, Our Girls (Pentland Press, 1995)
Demarne, Cyril, The London Blitz – A Fireman's Tale (Battle of Britain Prints International, 1991)
Ewen, Shane, Fighting Fires (Palgrave Macmillan, 2010)
Horner, John, Studies in Industrial Democracy (Gollancz, 1974)
Radford, Frederick R, Fetch the Engine (FBU, 1951)
Sugarman, Martin, Jewish Participation in the Fire Service in the Second World War (Vallentine Mitchell, 2016)

Primary sources
Firefighter magazine, from 1932 to the present.
FBU archive at the Modern Records Centre, Warwick University.
London Fire Brigade Museum – records and filmed interviews with firefighters.

"Firefighting really is a team activity. It means we need training departments, we need planning and we need technical knowledge to develop modern operational procedures. We need fire safety specialists. We need fire investigators. We need our emergency fire controls; the starting point for any emergency response. All firefighters ask is that they are able to do their job well; to have the support and resources they need in order to properly protect the communities they serve. Achieving that remains the mission of the Fire Brigades Union."

Matt Wrack, General Secretary, Fire Brigades Union